VERSE AFIRE

VERSE AFIRE

Volume 1

WALTER ERICKSON

Copyright © 2011 by Walter Erickson

ISBN 1456552694

This book was printed in the United States of America

A special dedication to Richard Fernandez, founder and writer of the best blog on the net, The Belmont Club. Wretchard, his nom de plume, posts every day on events of interest, to which I often address some verse. These verses and my added comments eventually appear on my blog Verse-afire. I believe it is fair to say that without Wretchard's posts on the Belmont Club most of these verses would not have been written. It goes without saying that neither Richard Fernandez nor the Belmont Club bear any responsibility for any of the words in this book.

TABLE OF CONTENTSi

MAY 2009. Three months into the Obama administration and already large parts of the country hoped for a change. On May 4th Verse-afire came into existence with the following rather innocuous verse about singing fish. I confess I wondered if I had enough material to write tomorrow's post. Somehow I did, and tomorrow followed tomorrow, for the world is full of things to write about, if one but looks for them.

SALMON CHANTED EVENING

I have stood on a lonely beach, listening to the gentle shushing of the waves, fishing the Atlantic Ocean in the deepness of the night, a translucent moon lighting the water, turning the sand to glittering bits of tiny diamonds. At such moments I care naught about catching fish, for I am waiting for the moon to set, waiting for the night to surround me, waiting for the fish to sing. For they do sing, but only to those who choose to hear them. Old standards, mostly.

Something's fishy, people say
A slur to briny cousins
You don't hear fish say that 'bout us
Though reasons they have dozens
We treat them all about the same
With hook and net and trawler
We bait them with some eel or squid
And sometimes a night crawler
And all because they're good to eat
Their taste is quite delicious
Salmon, trout or small mouth bass
Just show me where the fish is

1

They're not as dumb as some do think
They talk and sing till late
Nearer My Cod To Thee is one
And another Kiss Me Skate
Come Joe Sardine In My Flying Machine
And the popular Am l Blue
I love to hear those good old songs
But I sure wish they'd sing something new

MR. TALLYMAN

Pakistan announced it is building two large plutonium reactors, thus dramatically enlarging their nuclear warhead production capacity. To what end? A nuke super-store? Who would they sell the bombs to? Saudi Arabia? The Taliban? I suspect we know the answer.

Come Mr. Tallyman, tally me banana
Is now Come Mr. Taliban let me show you this
Nice little thing we've got here'n Pashtunanana
For the right price we are sure you cannot miss
Think of the joy you can bring to Muslim masses
Think of the laughter the Arab street will find
Think of the tears as you kick those Yankee asses
Think of the fears you will raise in Kaffir's mind
Don't think of price for we know you can afford it
We know you've got resources out the old kazoo
Just sign your name here and then we can record it
Then after that you'll just have to holler boo
Everyone knows that you never show no mercy
Everyone knows that you mean just what you say
One little bomb could take out all of New Jercy
Two little bombs and you own the USA
Come Mr. Taliban to Pashtunanana
Come Mr. Taliban cross my palm with gold
Come Mr. Taliban tally me banana
Soon everyone will be doing as he's told

3

BILL AND HILL

Former President Bill Clinton has just been named Special UN Envoy for Haiti. It seems the Clintons will always be with us. We know Bill's story, and how he got there, but what of Hillary? First Lady, Senator from New York, Secretary of State, none of which would have happened had she not married Bill. The true story of how Bill and Hillary met has not been told, except to me, by an acquaintance from Arkansas, who knew them back in the sweet used to be.

Young Hill, fresh out of school of law
While driving south for pleasure
Did chance to be in Arkansas
Which she thought was a treasure
She thought she'd stay a little while
But not for long, no, mercy
The backwoods didn't suit her style
But better than New Jercy
She thought she better get a job
A good one would be dandy
She asked a guy whose shirt said Bob
Who said see Bill or Randy
You'll find them in old Frank's Saloon
Most evenin's after dinner
You'll know them, Randy's a balloon
While Bill's a little thinner
She wondered what they did for funs
In woods so deep, my gracious
And stuffed a pair of tiny guns
Into her bra capacious
Inside she found a lookin' guy
A-grinnin' and a-leerin'

4

He fixed her with his wand'rin eye
So graciously endearin'
She said hello and might by chance
You're either Bill or Randy
I'm both he laughed and we can dance
To good old boy Moe Bandy
They spun the floor, her head awhirl
They danced the floor so lightly
She thought I'm just a college girl
He's holding me too tightly
And what is more he is for sure
So absolutely charming
And though I'm just the girl du jour
This feeling is alarming
She knew she had to pry him free
She'd have to try the pistols
She hated how he hummed off key
She didn't like the whistles
She pulled her guns, said you're too much
I like my men more strangerous
He grinned, said ah could tell by touch
Them mammalia was derringerous
You weren't all that scared, she said
Are guns in bras so normal
And with a grin he shook his head
Said not when goin' formal
He said a gal he sometimes saw
Who every woman hates
She always carried in her bra
A pair of 38s
They fell in love right then and there
To everyone a mystery
They pledged their lives they each would share
The rest, they say, is history

A MARVELOUS OPPORTUNITY

The London Times reports that one Ludwig Minelli, owner of a Swiss assisted suicide clinic, who describes death as a marvelous opportunity, has been investigated by the authorities regarding irregular financial profiting.

A marvelous opportunity, sir
He said with a winsome smile
With that I'm sure you will concur
Since we're here but little while
So why not take the chance to find
Some peace and quiet now
Your troubles we can help unwind
We'll smooth your troubled brow
This contract tells you what you get
We urge you read each line
For surely you'd not want to fret
That things were not condign
The Power of Attorney sir
A bit of legalese
That I am sure will not deter
Your wish to be at ease
Ah there we are, our task is done
Please lie down on this couch
The needle now, it's only one
There's never any ouch
The peace of death be unto you
We know your life's a wreck
Goodbye dear friend, and toodle-oo
And thank you for the check

FLY ME TO THE MOON

On Wednesday Iran conducted a missile test. The Sejil-2, an Intermediate Range Ballistic Missile with the range to reach Israel, launched successfully and landed in the northern Iranian desert without incident. The thing about the Sejil-2, apart from being the missile Ahmadinejad intends to use to destroy Israel once he has his bomb, is that it is powered by a solid fuel rocket motor that most experts believe came from Pakistan. The great Persian Empire of Ahmadinejad's dreams is incapable of inventing or building anything on its own, and even rocket motors need to be imported from, of all places, Pakistan. I believe Ahmadinejad is aware of this, and laments the fact that if he is to fly to the moon, it will be as a paying passenger on someone else's ship.

Fly me to the moon
Let me play among the stars
All I need's a rocket ship
To get me up to Mars
If only I could make the things
Right here at home but no
I've got to go to Pakistan
That's where I've got to go
A rocket motor's just beyond
Our skill set now alas
And so our missiles poop along
And just run out of gas
It's sad to think us Persians can't
Do things the Pakis can
Of course we also cannot make
A truck or a sedan
And come to think of it we're not

Too hot at trains and planes
Though pumping oil we're just as good
As Eskimos and Danes
We threaten people, stamp our feet
Make statements bold and brave
But getting missiles in the air
We can't our ass to save
Israelis laugh and point and joke
And sometimes even smirk
But they'll stop laughing if we can
Just get the thing to work

MOMMY! MOMMY!

The Mommy State is with us, as evidenced by the overwhelming number of women who voted for Barack Obama, as well as for the general state of the culture that is becoming more and more like France every day. Women are different from men, in that their first thought is the protection and maintenance of their children. Where once a woman depended on a man for these services, she now depends on the State, and so will continue to vote for those who agree to provide for them. Men are no longer needed. The State is now husband and master. But can it last?

We find us poised with quite a daunting thesis
An argument with which I must agree
When Mommy State implodes who gets the pieces
Is something I at present cannot see
In eighteen one a Brit named Alex Tyler
Proclaimed democracies not long to run
He didn't say it just to be a riler
He said that in the best case, number one
Democracies last only 'til the voters
Find out their votes breed governmental doles
He didn't know that once invented motors
That women could be driven to the polls
They voted in the guys who'd give them power
They're voting for them to this very day
They disengaged the cradle from the bower
And now we find we'll soon have hell to pay
The Mommy State has fastened on our culture
But surely it has finally run its course
That shadow overhead is from a vulture
Just waiting for some unforgiving force

9

To put a noisy end to all this posing
To see such nonsense put at last to bed
I see this lefty chapter quickly closing
If lucky we shall not have many dead
The Mommy State will last until some tragic
Event now clearly seen as tipping point
Will clean the slate again as if by magic
And once again the men will run the joint

MINISTRY OF TRUTH

The Obama Administration, in the person of Janet Napolitano, Secretary Homeland Security, has decreed that in the future terror attacks on the United States would not be described as terror attacks, but as man-made disasters. I don't remember President Obama appointing George Orwell to the Ministry of Truth, but I guess he did.

It's good to see a feminist
Admit that men exist
E'en though man-made disaster
Is a term the fems insist
Portrays the gender male in all
Its forms and histories
The wonder is they love us so
Just more life's mysteries
The problem though is greater than
Male gender understood
If she's the anti-terror czar
Then you would think she would
At least pretend that she believes
That people mean us harm
Instead she thinks the auras from
The O will be the charm
That coupled with our bowing down
And making real amends
Will steer them from the terror way
And make them lasting friends

WIR FAHREN GEGEN ENGELLAND

When the German battleship Bismarck sailed into the North Atlantic in May 1941, her sailors sang Wir Fahren Gegen Engelland (We Sail Against England). Little did they know it was to be a death cruise for most of them, for the British found the Bismarck and sank her. Are we, the United States, like the Bismarck, sailing on a death cruise? Are the Obama administration's economic and foreign policies driving us to a watery grave? Are we well on the way to what the radical left so fiercely desires, a toothless, bankrupt and humiliated America?

Wir fahren gegen Engelland!
The Bismarck's crew did sing
Wir fahren gegen Everyman!
Obama's cry doth ring
Everyone except of course
The unions large and small
As well as every other source
The Democrats can call
Their friends and allies who will give
Their votes and labor to
The rest of us will get the shiv
Thrust home by you know who
The North Koreans build their nukes
And threaten one and all
Say CIA and other spooks
We're heading for a fall
The State Department shakes its head
And issues reprimands
But by and large when all is said
We're sitting on our hands
Obama now owns all the stock

In Chrysler and GM
His health care plan's a laughingstock
Except to us and them
We'll soon be France or Sweden
If Obama has his way
'Cause there's no one here impedin'
His fierce drive to make us pay
For all the sins committed
By the US over time
There's no excuse permitted
We must pay for every crime
With fahren gegen Engelland
Still ringing in our ears
We watch Obama's fascist hand
And swallow down our fears

DON'T CALL ME, I'LL CALL YOU

The German magazine Der Spiegel has revealed that the International Tribunal looking into the assassination of Lebanon Prime Minister Rafik Hariri in 2005 has received information from an unnamed source that connects a cell phone used in the assassination to a man named Abd-al-Majid Ghamlush, a member of Hezbollah, and thus to Syria. All cell phones used in the attack were destroyed immediately after the assassination, but Ghamlush made the mistake of calling his girlfriend before destroying his, and he has as a consequence mysteriously disappeared.

Tribunal International knows
But somehow cannot find
The evidence that daily grows
(Perhaps they do not mind)
That some who live in Syria
With Hezbollahan pals
Did something, (I won't weary ya
With relevant detals)
That kinda sorta looks a lot
Like murder cruel and foul
But uncrossed t's and i's sans dot
Prevent them acting now
But Spiegel now has spilled the beans
On one Majid Ghamlush
Whose cell phone call was just the means
To make him sort of shush
For he has disappeared I fear
From his home town of Rumin
And we shall never ever hear
From him I am assumin'

In Syria they smile and say
We don't know naught what happen
We weren't there that awful day
In fact we were home nappin'
Meanwhile the boss Assad sits tight
(He loved Rafik Hariri)
And says these killings are not right
And questions make him weary

MAKING STUFF

Have you noticed we hardly actually make anything anymore? Oh, we make airplanes and high tech medical equipment, but we no longer make the little things people use every day, like shoes and waffle irons. Go to Wal-Mart and check the country of origin on the boxes. If we did, one day, want or have to start making stuff again, would anyone know how to do it?

Making stuff is all the rage
In countries far away
They work for a subsistence wage
A couple bucks a day
While here at home the folks pretend
They're working hard but they're
Just stacking paper end to end
To climb that corporate stair
No need to dirty up one's hands
By working with the soil
No, building things on shifting sands
Is what we now call toil
We've built a nice society
Where everyone's a king
But soon will come sobriety
'Cause we don't build a thing
That ordinary people want
That people really need
Who wants to work, that's just a stunt
What's real is wholesome greed
What's that you say, it's coming down?
Just watch it all collapse?
Oh well, we've had our time in town
The kids will pay, perhaps

THE LABYRINTH

The National Archives reports a one terabyte storage disk, enough to hold a million novels, is missing, taken or lost sometime between October 2008 and January 2009. Richard Fernandez, at the Belmont Club, calls the search for it Entering The Labyrinth. Was it stolen? If so, who profits, politically or financially? If it was stolen, who would pay for the information?

Knossos was a lively town
Or so the ancients say
Its splendor gained it great renown
A marvel of its day
But gods are mortal after all
And fall in love with bulls
And thus was born what we would call
A monster dressed in wools
His body man, a bull for head
Poor Minos was distraught
His wife, the goddess he had wed
Dishonor on him brought
And so was built the labyrinth
To house the half-man beast
With name inscribed upon a plinth
In letters deeply creased
Good Theseus did undertake
To slay the monster dead
But first precautions he must make
By stringing out a thread
Behind to lessen the great risk
For Minotaur lay hid
In deep recess with missing disk
A terabyte for bid

ADRIFT

The world is changing, and with it the United States. Where once was stability and shared values, there now is bitter divide. Where once was rule of law, there now is judicial fiat. Where once we knew who we were, we now question who we are. Where once we were proud, we now are told we must be ashamed. The world has changed, and so have we. We are no longer who we were. It is an open question as to whether we will ever again be proud and confident. Or is this a passing phase, a moment of inattention, to be remedied by a future generation more sure of themselves.

Here there be tygers
The olde mappes once said
Then came the British
Who painted them red
All that is gone now
That world is no more
We've come to the place
Where there's no welcome shore
The currents won't take us
Where we want to go
The winds that once shapened
The world that we know
No longer blow fairly
But fitful and wild
We recognize barely
The world that we've styled
Can we recapture
That time and that way
I guess that's the question
Before us today

MISSILES, SCHMISSILES

President Obama, in addition to proposing the cancellation of the F-22 program, the only fighter now in our inventory that can fight and defeat the newest Russian fighters, fighters that Russia is busily exporting to our enemies, also proposes drastically reduced funding for the missile shield designed to protect us against rogue strikes from regimes such as North Korea and Iran. Since Obama has already declared that terror attacks will no longer be called terror attacks, but Man Made Disasters, and The War On Terror has been renamed Overseas Contingencies, I assume North Korea and Iran are no longer considered enemies, but Friends Who Have Yet To Embrace Us. With the missile shield down, and Iran and North Korea building nukes and missiles, we must hope that Obama's charm will deflect any incoming.

Regardless of the fact it's late
I sit here contemplating fate
The news from DC sits not well
And so I take up pen to tell
How horrified I am to hear
That O has canceled what I fear
Will one day prove to be our sole
Defense against Islamist goal
Of taking our fair country down
And driving us into the ground
With missiles tipped with warheads that
Will get to us in nothing flat
Where is that famous missile shield
That Bush and Reagan had us wield
It's gone for O said come what may
That it's not needed. Let us pray

FRANKENSTEIN'S MONSTER

The United Nations is now ruled by the Organization of the Islamic Conference, which passed the Cairo Declaration On Human Rights that stated all human rights and freedoms must be subject to Islamic law, that is, Sharia. The OIC routinely gets UN resolutions passed condemning Israel, the United States, and anyone else they disagree with. The 57 nation Muslim bloc's most recent attempt to destroy the right of free speech of non-muslims consists of a UN resolution that labels any disagreement with Islam as hate speech. The people who pay the bills for this nonsense, we the American taxpayer, have virtually no say in what the UN does and says. I don't think that is what was intended.

Dr Frankenstein did dream
Of monsters to create
And in his eye a simple gleam
That one day he'd be great
In '45 that dream came true
As nations far and wide
Urged by the old red white and blue
Got on board for the ride
United Nations it was called
Though united it was not
And from the first it truly galled
As crooks and swindlers got
A seat at the big table next
To guys who foot the bill
Who pretty soon were sorely vexed
And wished that they could kill
The monster they had wished to be
A symbol of world peace

But turned into a foaming sea
Of trouble without cease
If Dr Frankenstein were here
He'd sure know what to do
He'd shove a great big sharpened spear
Right up the old kazoo

WHAT, ME WORRY?

Secretary of Defense Gates, touring the Middle East, is assuring the Saudis and other allies that the Obama administration is not throwing them under the bus with the coming talks with Iran. They are, curiously, not reassured.

Why should you worry, Gates said with a smile
We're with you and always have been
Of course just because we've been friends for a while
Does not mean we think you are kin
The US is under new management now
We have an agenda or two
Don't ask us the why or the when or the how
Don't ask us if it includes you
We know what we're doing, we know what we know
We know that Iran is a friend
So friendly we feel that our friendship must show
A regard for their nuclear end
We've outlawed the terror, it's no longer here
Attacks are disasters man made
That being the case you have nothing to fear
You all have it made in the shade
Of course history shows that appeasements don't work
That appeasers are seen to be weak
That sooner or later there'll be a Dunkirk
And it's happening now as we speak

WHO'S COUNTING?

The Inspector General of the Federal Reserve, when asked where all the trillions of dollars lent or spent by the Federal Reserve went, replied she didn't keep track of that. I wonder if anybody does.

Don't you really think it's funny
That the people with the money
Would at least know where the heck it all got sent
But when you ask about it
Then you might as well just shout it
'Cause the only thing they know is it got spent
Spent on whom you might well wonder
Spent it well or just a blunder
They just shrug their shoulders with a winning smile
Saying please now not to worry
Things just happen in a hurry
We'll get back to you in just a little while
If there's one thing I am certain
It is time to pull the curtain
On the IG at the Federal Reserve
As the trillion debt is mounting
She just shrugs and says who's counting
So I guess we always get what we deserve

C'MON, GET HAPPY!

Far too many of us are feeling unusually doleful these days, as if the world as we know and knew it is about to go under. The government taking over the auto industry? The President of the United States firing the president of General Motors, a private company? Both those things are the very definition of fascism. The budget deficits and national debt climbing to unsustainable levels? The Chinese warning us not to debase our currency? Both those things are the very definition of economic lunacy. We have much to be doleful about, but keep the faith, the country will still be here in 2010, when the people who don't think about politics will turn out the guys they see as the authors of all their troubles, and vote in the other guys. That's the way it works.

Forget your troubles come on get happy
Chirped a song of the 30s back then
No matter the lyric was sappy
The point was that women and men
Who looked on the dark side of living
With joblessness, hard times and strife
Need someone prepared to be giving
Them reason to treasure their life
So that's why I write these here verses
To say that the gloom is misplaced
It's bad but the thing that is worse is
To think it's the worst thing we've faced
We're not on the brink of disaster
We're not going over the cliff
If cheerful we're out of it faster
This bad time will be just a riff
In this opera bouffe we're all watching

As Obama and crew crash and burn
The voters the drift they are catching
And soon it will be adults turn
There are those who will sob it and bawl it
I ask you, don't be one of those
'Cause in truth I don't know whatcha call it
But it's mighty darn sure lachrymose

DOUBLESPEAK

Why do the Obama legions give him a pass when he says things with which they disagree? The answer is that they know he is not telling the truth, that he is being disingenuous for political reasons. Barack Obama had previously endorsed same sex marriage, yet when he stated during last year's presidential campaign that he was opposed to it, homosexual activists gave him a pass. The radical left and the unions, both of whom hate Nafta, winked and nodded when Obama spoke in favor of it. Why are his supporters serene in the face of statements they disagree with? Because they know he doesn't mean it.

I love him so, the young thing thrilled
He's cool and young and handsome
So what if verity is killed
And truth be held for ransome?
The journalist with glazey stare
Will tell all who will listen
There's nothing like the brilliant glare
Of halo's golden glisten
The ardent cling to every word
They gasp at all inflection
And then discuss what they have heard
Without the least reflection
They love him so for what he says
And what he doesn't say
They love the eyes that truly mes
Merize in every way
And most of all they love to hear
The truth as he has seen it
But through it all one thing is clear
He really doesn't mean it

26

WHERE'S THE FIZZ?

There was a time people listened when the President of the United States spoke. That time has past. President Obama has misread President Teddy Roosevelt's insistence that the United States walk softly but carry a big stick. No one fears or pays attention to President Obama, who walks softly and carries a big smile. North Korea detonates a nuke, knowing we will do nothing. The Iranians continue to build nukes, knowing we will do nothing. It is truly said, you can get more with a gun and a kind word than you can with just a kind word.

The mullahs say, you wish we'd stop?
Whatever do you mean?
You used to be the biggest cop
But now you're truly seen
For what you are, a toothless boy
Come begging for to please
Your cringing manner brings us joy
And puts us at our ease
We've told you many times before
Our nukes are not for hold
We'll go ahead and build our store
If we may be so bold
We know you try to do your best
To look so rough and tough
But we know you won't pass the test
Big smiles just aint enough
But Bibi now's, a different guy
He's told you where to go
He's knows what's up, he isn't shy
He's gonna strike a blow
But we think we are ready for

Whatever Bibi does
We think that we can win this war
We think so just becuz
We know whose side that you are on
We know just where you stand
We know Barack is no Sharon
We know he'll lend no hand
To either side, that's who he is
He's just above all that
Where once US made soda fizz
Today the soda's flat

JUNE 2009 dawned brightly. The Phillies were World Champions and seemed likely to go back to the World Series. Meanwhile, overseas, on the anniversary of D-Day, British Prime Minister Gordon Brown gave a speech reflecting on the courage of the American soldirs at Obama Beach.

OBAMA BEACH

On June sixth, the anniversary of the D-Day landings, Gordon Brown, Prime Minister of Great Britain, gave a speech during the ceremonies at Omaha Beach, scene of great courage and carnage that fateful day in 1944, and called it Obama beach. There are those who believe the reference to be a slip of the tongue, easily made. There is, after all, little difference between Omaha and Obama. And to the mind of Gordon Brown, there is little difference between what was accomplished that day in 1944 and what the anointed one has accomplished sixty-five years later. Gordon Brown is a believer in the magic of Barack Obama, and what better way to acknowledge that magic than to re-name this hallowed beach in memory of the greatest president the United States has ever had or ever will have.

To those who think 'twas but a gaffe
I bid you think again, sir
Brown did not do it for a laugh
He did it for the men, sir
Who came ashore that fateful morn
And stumbled up the shingle
And raced across the bullet torn

29

Cruel beach, their nerves a-tingle
With just one thought upon their minds
To do this for Obama
A man they knew had future binds
To cure their country's trauma
Of self-inflicted anomie
Beset with doubt and worry
So with a smart economy
They ran as in a hurry
To hasten and prepare the way
For the one blessed by the gods
Who'd take the reins on one fair day
Despite tremendous odds
And lead us all to heaven's gate
The land of milk and honey
Of course we'll have a while to wait
'Cause he's spent all of our money

MUSLIM INVENTIONS

In his speech in Cairo the other day, President Obama proudly proclaimed the Muslims invented the compass, printing, algebra, and the university. None of this is true. Europeans invented the university, the Chinese invented printing and the magnetic compass, and the Hindus of northern India invented algebra and the system of mathematics we use today, including the so-called Arabic numbers. Why do we call them Arabic numbers? Because when the Arabs conquered northern India they brought the mathematical systems invented by the Hindus back home with them. So I guess that's something. They at least recognized the Hindu math was better than what they were using. What other wonders did this marvelous civilization invent? Why, according to the American left, just about everything.

Wilbur and Orville, two Bedouin chaps
Believed that if Allah so willed
They could make a machine that would fly them, perhaps
Though they knew there's a chance they'd be killed
No matter the risk, no matter the peril
For Allah they'd do what it took
They flew a straight line, they flew in a curl
Then told all the world in a book
In Cairo a smart man, al-Bert was his name
Said gravity bends passing light
Then took off for Princeton and cashed in his fame
When Allah proved that he was right
A young man named Henry, while dining as planned
In the town of as-Sembly on kine
Threw a bone to a dog, drawing marks in the sand
And created the as-Sembly line

And thus so it went, and thus so it goes
That Muslims created it all
From fire to atoms, from heads to our toes
We owe it to them to recall
That without the great Arab advances to date
The world would indeed be so poor
That we'd witness the famine and terrible state
Of the masses lay crushed at our door
All hail to the Arabs, those masters of art
And science and math and the lot
Who sit in the sand by their fire and fart
Eating goat from the communal pot

DOWN THE LOO

Monday, the first of June, 2009, is a date that very well might be remembered for some time, for it is the date the United States ceased being a capitalist economy. The forced bankruptcy of Chrysler by the Federal government and the threats to Chrysler bondholders were the start, but the forced GM bankruptcy under terms favorable to the United Auto Workers union is far more troubling. The Federal government, under the leadership of President Barack Obama, has moved the country down the road to socialism. The Federal government now owns 60% of General Motors, in the process giving the United Auto Workers everything they ever dreamed of getting. The UAW now owns 7.5% of whatever is left of GM, 800,000 retired UAW workers will continue to have all their health care and pension costs paid for, and the Obama administration has agreed to ban the sale in the US of all foreign cars not made in the United States. The man President Obama placed in charge of overseeing the GM bankruptcy is a 31 year old who has never held a job in the private sector, knows nothing about automobiles or finance, but who has the only qualification necessary – he's a left wing Democrat activist, having worked previously for George Soros. Hugo Chavez, the Venezuelan nutcase, has said the next book he's going to give Obama is Lenin's What Is To Be Done. That will make two copies in the Obama family library.

How do I love thee, let me count the ways,
Are the opening words of Liz to her sweet love
But how did I lose thee, after just one hundred days

Are words we cry beseeching God above
To turn the glass, reverse the sand
Don't let the country slide to the abyss
Give us the strength to make a stand
And save us from Obama's deadly kiss
Who are they who gave us such
A radical as ever wore the cloak
Of hope and change who promised oh so much
And turned around to be the cruelest joke
The laugh's on us who thought that we
Were safe from all those leftist twists and turns
We thought that there could never be
A day we'd sit and watch as country burns
One hundred days is all it took
To nationalize the banks and autos too
The plan, my friends, is quite an open book
He plans to stuff the country down the loo

CAPITALISM, AVE ATQUE VALE

It was announced Tuesday that Chrysler is out of bankruptcy. The deal, as dictated by the Obama administration, calls for the Italian carmaker Fiat to own 35% of Chrysler, the United Auto Workers union 55%, and the US and Canadian governments 10%. Is the forced deal constitutional? No. Does it matter? No. I have never seen, nor did I ever expect to see, a president of the United States so openly and brazenly throw aside the law in order to reward his UAW friends, both with Chrysler and General Motors. Bankruptcy law is settled law, the law of the land, but that did not deter the Obama administration from telling the first creditors, the Chrysler bond holders, that contrary to law the UAW union would get first dibs and the bond holders would take what the president said they would take, which was 29 cents on the dollar. When the bond holders complained they were threatened, so they took it, figuring if they didn't they would get nothing. Can you imagine the screams of outrage and calls for impeachment had George W. Bush done that? Yet the media is silent, complicit in the unlawful actions of the one they adore.

The UAW put up no money but got 55% of the new Chrysler/Fiat corporation by agreeing to pick up the legacy benefits and health care costs of the workers. Fiat got 45% of the new Chrysler/Fiat corporation by agreeing to give Chrysler its technology in small cars and small engines, a combination the American buying public has consistently said it does not want and will not buy. Fiat has an even lower score in customer satisfaction than Chrysler. Has anyone on this side of the Atlantic ever bought a Fiat? So after the forced Obama Chrysler bankruptcy, the two principal owners of the new Chrysler put up not one red cent for 90% of the company, and the American taxpayer, who put up billions in loans and outright gifts, gets to share the remaining 10% with Canada. Now we know why President Obama is always smiling; it's two down and Ford to go. All of which raises the question: Is what Obama has done to General Motors and Chrysler, and what he has done to the economy by putting the country in debt to the tune of trillions of dollars a year into the foreseeable future, incompetence or design?

Walter Chrysler built his cars
With care and keen attention
To see that style and detail mars
Got hardly any mention
Until that is the union halls
Took over car production
With worker rights and work rule calls
And quality reduction
But times were fat so no one cared
That wages were a-soaring
And no one in his right mind dared
To think of underscoring
The risks of competition from
The Japanese and Germans
Get beat? they smiled, they're just too dumb
Those Takeos and Hermans
Now Walter Chrysler is no more
No more is General Motors
The president chalked up the score
And charged it to the voters
Then put in charge one of his czars

A man who said he doesn't
Know a thing 'bout building cars
But criticize we mustn't
We have to ask, what does this mean
Why all this rearranging
The socialists are on the scene
Our country they are changing
It's ave atque vale tears
It's hello and goodbye
To all we knew, now still your fears
We have in charge a guy
Who takes us down that frightful path
To ruin and decay
Just look at it, just do the math
We're soon at judgment day
Hail and farewell to all we knew
They work while we all dally
Ring out the old, ring in the new
It's ave atque vale

AN UNDISCLOSED LOCATION

A few days ago a US drone strike in northern Pakistan killed a number of Pakistani Taliban. As the mourners gathered for the funeral some days later, another drone struck the funeral, killing three top Taliban commanders and between fifty and seventy rank and file Taliban, the number dependent on which source you believe. The already dead Taliban were not further harmed. The head Taliban guy, the top commander of the Pakistani Taliban, Baitullah Mehsud, attended the funeral, but according to some sources survived the attack. We shall see. You may recall that a few months ago the very same Baitullah Mehsud called the AP from an undisclosed location and boasted of the ruin he was about to rain on the United States and all its minions. The question is, since he called the AP from an undisclosed location, is he now also in an undisclosed location, dispersed by the drone strike over a square kilometer or two of Pakistani scrub.

Baitullah Mehsud was an angry man
Who called up the AP
To claim that he and his mates can
And will claim victory
He said he would amaze the world
With blows to the great satan
And claimed that death about him swirled
And terror lay a'waitin'
He sneered our fear hangs like a pall
And terror's his vocation
But notice that he made the call
From an undisclosed location
But just because you're undisclosed
Won't mean you're unlocated

Not if the US is disposed
To make your life truncated
The silent death from out the sky
Sought out the funeral party
The missiles flew and bye and bye
The men who once were hearty
Were just as dead as were their friends
Whose passing they were mourning
Struck down by those who sought their ends
Attacking without warning
A job well done we all would say
Good job from top to bottom
But did Mehsud escape that day?
I think we finally got him

YOU CAN'T NEGOTIATE WITH A DEAD TERRORIST

A month or so ago the Sri Lankan army cornered the remnants of the rebel Tamil Tigers and killed them all. Various and sundry Western voices expressed dismay, exclaiming that by killing them they left no one to negotiate with. A spokeswoman for Chatham House, a British NGO, was particularly upset that the Sri Lankan army brutally ended the forty year war with the even more brutal Tamil Tigers by doing it the old fashioned way, by killing them, and expressed their outrage in no uncertain terms. I have thought about this strange way of thinking, and have come to a reluctant conclusion. It seems wars are no longer to be won, but negotiated into a kind of perpetual conflict, in which neither side is defeated, and the casualty count keeps climbing, despite the valiant efforts by such as Chatham House to ameliorate the suffering.

Thank God there were no NGOs
Around in Patton's day
For they'd have tried him, goodness knows
For getting in the way
Of all good Germans whom they felt
Would likely stop the war
And all good Nazis would be dealt
With kindly, as before
But no, George Patton told his men
The enemy must die
So his Third Army figured then
That Generals do not lie
They cranked up all their Shermans
And in weather bleak and fine

They killed their share of Germans
And they cracked the Siegfried line
So Hodges, Simpson, George and Ike
Killed Germans by the score
They did what NGOs don't like
They went and won the war
But not today, for goodness sake
The New York Times would frown
If someone on our side would take
The chance to mow them down
And turn his guns on men who try
To kill us every day
It's not for us to reason why
It's just for us to pay
The price in blood the left insists
Is penance for our sins
And they would have us slash our wrists
And cheer when bad guy wins

Things must have looked grim indeed in the Spring of 2009 regarding the Middle East, the Iranian bomb and the Israeli response. No, the Israeli Air Force did not fly in the summer of 2009, nor in the summer of 2010. But the summer of 2011? It all depends on whether or not the Iranians are committed to national suicide and explode a bomb, for the only way you know a nuclear bomb works is to test it. And when they do, there will be more than one mushroom cloud in the neighborhood.

THE 300

Israel yesterday, Sunday, held a nationwide civil defense test, getting ready for the inevitable war with Iran. The Obama initiative to Teheran will shortly be seen to be spun sugar. Bibi will not wait for the inevitable. He will strike Iran before the summer is out. And what then of the Obama olive branch when the missiles start to fly and the Middle East is aflame? Obama simply does not want to believe that the mullahs want the Israelis dead, and after them, us. Bibi will not let the Persians get the bomb, even if an Iranian bomb is okay with Obama. The only question in my mind is, is Netanyahu Leonidas? Does Ahmadinejad think he's Xerxes? Does Western civilization once again hinge on a small group of guys with guts, this time the Israeli Air Force and 300 F-16s?

Netanyahu takes no guff
We know the man is something tough
He'll not forget what happened to his brother
He'll take his time to get it right
But no mistake, the man will fight

One holocaust they've had, but not another
The mullahs in Teheran now squirm
As Israel now has a firm
And steady hand upon the Ship of State
When Bibi says they shall not get
The bomb then it's a darn good bet
The IAF will fly without debate
The F15s and F16s
Have long range tanks and so that means
The range has been increased to let them reach
The mullahs and their scurvy crew
And hidden bomb assemblies too
Though all know it won't be a day at beach
The IAF is set to fly
The crews all know the reason why
It's all because the mullahs raised the stakes
The threat to kill the Jews is real
And that is why the pilots feel
They'll fly to hell and back if's what it takes
Who knows what the result will be
Who knows what horrors we will see
When Persians block the Straits of old Hormuz
And US Navy gets the job
Of taking out the Persian mob
Unless of course Obama wants to lose
With Persia on the rise again
They think they have the guts and men
Like Xerxes thought when facing but a few
Three hundred Spartans laid them low
Three hundred planes to strike the blow
We're gonna see Thermopylae number Two

Coming up on two years later nothing much has changed.

AMATEURS TALK TACTICS

The United States currently has about 49,000 troops in Afghanistan, with a projected 68,000 troops in theater by the end of the year. Nato has about another 32,000 troops in Afghanistan, mostly non-combat troops, or combat troops like the Germans whose government does not permit them to shoot unless first shot at. All these forces sit at the end of a vulnerable 1,200 mile long supply line from the port of Karachi, across Pakistan, through the Khyber Pass, and into Afghanistan, ending at Kabul or Kandahar. We have already lost a valuable air base in Kyrgyzstan, and we and Nato are examining other routes through Russia and elsewhere. But what happens if Pakistan implodes, what happens if the Taliban succeed in making the supply route untenable, what happens if these alternate routes do not become available? What happens if our army is cut off, relying on air re-supply like the Germans at Stalingrad?

I think we've seen this one before
Let me think now, just which war
Was ended when the guys on the high ground
Surrounded those encamped below
And pressed them till they hollered whoa
As guns up in the hills threw round 'pon round
Of course it's happened many times
In many years and many climes
That armies get cut off and then they die
But that won't happen to our guys

44

Our civvie leaders are too wise
And we must never ask the reason why
We have secure lines of supply
Another reason I know why
Our guys are safe in far Pashtunistan
Our leaders simply would not dare
To leave our guys defenseless there
Adrift, surrounded in some foreign land
The Paki guys in ISI
Are operating on the sly
To see the Taliban and all that crew
Take Pakistan and all their nukes
They care not all for our rebukes
They'll take the land and have Sharia too
And then they all will turn on us
Egged on by Chinese and the Russ
And then some big decisions will be made
Do we pull out and wash our hands
Or do we take out all the Stans
Whichever, there's a price that must be paid
A price that's paid in blood right now
Or later paid no matter how
Much spinning out the truth our leaders spin
To take Vienna we must be
Prepared to fight to victory
'Cause once you start to fight you better win

ON BENDED KNEE

President Obama's speech today in Cairo will focus upon
three things: Obama's Muslim upbringing; America's
historical enmity toward Islam; and the Jews. I cannot
predict he will be able to hold himself in check and not
again bow before an Arab king, but I can confidently
predict he will blame the United States for all the
troubles of the world, and ask forgiveness. In fact, these
are not predictions, but certainties, for Verse-afire has
come into possession, I shall not say how, of an advance
copy of President Obama's speech. Curiously, it rhymes.

O land of Ra! O land of ancient stones!
We come to beg forgiveness for our sins
We hope our being here somewhat atones
For all we've done to loose the awful djinns
That harmed you and your children all your life
Like medicine and science and our cash
Those awful things that lead to constant strife
And turn the flame of life to cindered ash
We beg of you to please not turn away
We need your guidance and your counsel now
On bended knee I plead with you this day
To teach us Allah's way and your know how
For only when we've turned our faith to yours
Will God's work here on Earth be truly won
And highest form of art is local tours
And all bow down to Ra the god of sun
O land of Ra! The pharaohs' gracious land!
Thy glories down the ages ring in ears
Together we must travel hand in hand
To spread Islamic kindness through the years

I've come today to ask you pretty please
To think not ill of us here by your side
I'm sure my words have put you at your ease
By saying West Bank Jews we can't abide
The land of Palestine is truly yours
The Jews so long ago had moved away
They're back and must be put down on all fours
The entity sha'nt live another day
There's work to do before we say goodbyes
Israeli force and terror must be o'er
Hamas and Hezbollah are just good guys
Who want their place on earth however poor
Hold hands with us the people of the West
And help us understand the Muslim mind
Your truthfulness and kindness are the best
In Islam you will find no other kind
In parting I will leave you with one thought
You have a friend in DC and it's me
You've heard I'm sure the US can be bought
But save your dough, I'm giving it for free

HE WENT THATAWAY

Congressman Charley Rangle, D-NY, was in the news recently, half-jokingly advising President Obama not to come to Harlem without proper ID, since to do so might lead him to being shot by a white cop, Obama being, you know, black. Charley Rangle has always, to my mind, been one of the good guys, not a hater like some of his Democrat colleagues, but more interested in the perks associated with being a powerful politician. You may recall a few months ago Charley was found to be a tax cheat, like so many Democrats, and explained his failure to pay his taxes on his being unable to understand the tax code, which is mildly humorous, since Congressman Rangel chairs the powerful House committee that writes the tax rules for the rest of us. You might think being found to be a tax cheat would cause someone shame, might cause that someone to feel he could not show his face again in polite society, but you would be wrong about that, at least as it applies to Charley Rangel. He has no trouble riding into town, even though he knows the sheriff has a Wanted poster in his office with Charley's picture on it, and words TAX CHEAT in big, black letters.

> The sheriff moseyed up the street
> Boots kicking up the sand
> The Wanted poster of the cheat
> Gripped firmly in his hand
> He'd seen that face ride into town
> And head for the saloon
> A smiling face, a tiny frown
> The time was just high noon
> A-past the swinging doors he strode

His six-gun at his hip
A-past the horse the stranger rode
Still sweaty from the trip
He saw his quarry in the dark
A-standin' at the bar
His voice commanded in a bark
Just stand right where you are!
I've come here to arrest you, sir
For cheating on your taxes
You'll spend a goodly time in stir
Depending what the max is
The man looked up and smiled a smile
Said you know who I am?
It's well for you I do not rile
Or you'd be in a jam
For I'm beloved Congressman
Chuck Rangle from New York
And I'm the guy who writes the plan
For guys like you who work
Must follow under pain of law
The penalties are clear
No matter how quick is your draw
You'll serve at least a year
But none of this applies to me
Because, son, I'm your better
So you can not arrest me, see
But you can write me a letter
With that he put his shot glass down
And climbed upon his horsey
And headed north for New York town
Though he'd have to cross New Jorsey

SECRETARY OF DEFERENCE

I'm beginning to feel we don't need a Secretary of Defense so much as we need a Secretary of Deference. President Obama insists on apologizing for what he considers the sins of America's recent past, by which he means the actions of his predecessor, actions and policies designed to protect the lives and interests of the American people, and that of course makes those actions and policies immoral to all good liberal Democrats. North Korea explodes a nuclear bomb and our State Department issues a statement of regret. Such statements surely make the North Koreans shake in their boots, though I'm not so sure the shaking is not from laughter.

The Norks set off a nuclear blast
Without a by your leave
Our leaders say they are aghast
That Kim would so deceive
Us when we have assured him that
We're friends now, don't you see
No more the Bush Cheney diktat
We've goodies for you, free
And yes we know it's all our fault
That you act as you do
We thought your testing you would halt
If we were nice to you
We really don't know what to say
Nor how we should react
To how you're forcing us to pay
For our own suicide pact
Our Secretary of Deference says
We are saddened now to see
The PRK just won't take yes

For answer and so we
Must take a firmer stand and let
The North Koreans know
That we'll not let the sun to set
Before we strike a blow
For peace and honor and that stuff
And so we say today
That a strong note should be enough
To make the Kim folk pay
They only want attention so
Ignore and we'll be fine
So long as we don't mention though
Their crossing of the line
For nothing makes them crosser than
For us to criticize
The actions of the little man
Who leads them till he dies

COOLING TOWERS

In his suck-up to the Muslim world Thursday, President Obama stated Iran was entitled to generate electricity through nuclear power. But he knows and we know the Iranian nuclear program has nothing to do with generating electrical power, but with generating military power, namely the power to destroy Israel, an eventuality President Obama is apparently comfortable with. When Ahmadinejad smiles and says they are only building cooling towers, the cooling towers he has in mind are the burnt out skyscrapers of Tel-Aviv. Yet it is Israel President Obama is putting pressure on, not Iran. When the Iranian mullahs get that nuke, when they obliterate Israel, when another six million Jews die in a second holocaust, President Obama will have some reflecting to do, reflecting that may go something like this:

Iran has nukes, what's that you say?
I really can't believe that they
Would do a thing like that behind our backs
I've trusted them to tell the truth
About their nuclear plans, forsooth
And for my pains took lots of dirty cracks
From awful people on the right
Who seem to think it's time to fight
The peaceful mullahs and their lawful plans
To generate some AC power
By building a nice cooling tower
And sending juice out to the desert clans
I see no harm in such a scheme
I say let them fulfill their dream
Of climbing to the modern world with us
I am aware what they've been saying

That soon Israelis will be paying
For all the times they've hit us with the bus
But when friend Ahmadinejad
Promised I his word had had
I knew my charm and smile had won the day
So what if Haifa is no more
And Tel Aviv a burning sore
The important thing is peace is on the way

MEN OF STEEL

D-Day, the sixth of June, has passed quietly in the West. Too quietly. We tend not to notice these ancient reminders of past glories these days. Our attention is fixed not on survival, but on other, more important, things. The men who went ashore that day, onto a hostile beach, onto a hostile continent, are far removed from us in time and space, for they knew who they were, they knew what they were fighting for, and more importantly, they knew what they were fighting for was important. Not so today, when far too many of us here in the West believe nothing is worth fighting for, that there is no difference between us and the people who are trying to kill us, no difference between people who kill little girls and cut off heads before the camera and a society that poured water up the noses of three terrorists in order to forestall further attack. We have lost our way, lost our nerve, lost our souls, and before long we will have lost our country.

The Western world is dead and gone
And with it any sense
Of waking to a peaceful dawn
Of striking warlike tents
The Taliban, those bearded men
So brave when beating girls
Have dazzled our fair left again
Who love their glistening curls
The North Koreans built their bomb
Without a word from us
We greeted it with rare aplomb
And counted it a plus
That Mr. Kim agreed to take
More money and more oil

When he agreed no nukes to make
And wrapped us in his coil
Iran will shortly have the means
To kill six million Jews
While we put out behind the scenes
That really isn't news
Where once men fought for home and hearth
Now men fight not at all
For cultures that have lost their worth
Where duty does not call
Where have they gone, our men of steel?
Who saw things rearranged?
It isn't they who seem unreal
It's only us who've changed

MONEY MONEY MONEY

President Obama has outlined his strategy for gracefully ending the black mood of depression his presidency has plunged the country into without admitting he had anything to do with it. "It's like we do in Chicago," Rahm Emanuel said. "Money cures everything, and it will cure this. When things look darkest, that is when we in Chicago shine, for in the dark is when we are most graceful. The President has informed the Treasury that the printing presses will melt if need be, for he is determined to see everyone in this country has an organically grown chicken in every pot and a plug-in hybrid car in every garage." Press Secretary Robert Gibbs, at an informal press conference with several radical Muslim groups, laughed at the suggestion that the United States was abandoning its principles. "This Administration," Mr. Gibbs quipped, "will never abandon its principals. Get it? Principals. With an "a". Or its teachers, either. What's with you guys? I know you're laughing, I can see your beards move." But it isn't funny. The money spent so far is so mind bogglingly staggering, that I wonder if there was ever any real money involved at all. A thousand years ago the Chinese invented paper money. Money was no longer something valuable in itself, like a gold or silver coin, but a promissory note that said when presented to the proper authority it would be redeemed for the value stated on its face. The Chinese had invented the illusion of money, and nothing's been the same since.

It isn't paranoid to say
That what we see's disturbing
When markets start to act this way

It means something's perturbing
The way free markets operate
When all is hokey dokey
But when the pols don't play it straight
They should be in the pokey
They're not, of course, and I should state
The tycoon money lenders
And others who facilitate
The Congress's big spenders
Should join the crooks in durance vile
Their names be changed to numbers
But that will only happen while
We're dreaming in our slumbers
The Congress votes a pork fed bill
Without a thought or worry
Most people didn't care, but still
Some wondered what's the hurry
I think the Congress knew full well
That what they did was harmful
They gave to friends, but what the hell
Who took it by the armful
But here's the problem, if we look
It really wasn't euros
But just some numbers in a book
A-sitting in some bureaus
Until somewhere someplace some time
Someone needs some Jacksons
And writes a check or drops a dime
And initiates some actions
And somewhere a computer coughs
And numbers change direction
And offs are ons and ons are offs
In infinite collection
The point is no one ever sees

The actual pound or dollar
They might as well be wind in trees
A-blowing down a holler
There never was no dough to keep
It's all a sham and mirrors
For some of us are just the sheep
While others are the shearers

MIRANDA RIGHTS

We're all getting a little bloody minded, and with reason. Muslim terrorists continue to kill people every day, whether a young US soldier at a recruiting station in the United States or staging a slaughter in Mumbai, India, and have just blown up a hotel in Peshawar, Pakistan, killing many innocent civilians. We hear now that the Obama administration has decided to read captured terrorist killers their Miranda rights, telling them they have a right to remain silent and that we will provide them a lawyer if they cannot afford one. Of course, Mr. Holder's Justice Department is deeply concerned with the rights of terrorist killers. You may recall it was not so many years ago that Mr. Holder released many Puerto Rican terrorists in order to gain votes for Hillary Clinton's run for the Senate from New York, so Mr. Holder's views on terrorism are well known. Still, there is a way to get the job done properly while still reading the killers their Miranda rights. These terrorists are not afraid of death, they willingly and happily blow themselves up, believing they will be instantly in Paradise with 72 beautiful virgins, but there is one thing that terrifies them, and that is to be buried wrapped in a pig skin, for that would send them straight to hell. I propose, therefore, that we read them not their Miranda rights, but their Oscar Mayer rights. Wrap them in bacon, shoot them, and then read them their Miranda rights.

> The Justice Department is quakin'
> In fear that our soldiers be takin'
> It into their head
> To fill them with lead
> Before their Mirandas be makin'

I like the idea of bacon
The thought has the jihadists shakin'
Let's not wait till they're dead
Grab the bastards instead
Shove the stuff up their ass while they're wakin'

While a plea for his life he is makin'
Just grin with a little head shakin'
Then a shot to his head
Put the bastard to bed
And another in case he is fakin'

Mr. Holder says steps will be takin'
To prevent such a vile undertakin'
But our guys know that they
Are the ones who will pay
For the folly that Justice is makin'

THE DAYS GO SLOW BUT THE YEARS GO FAST

We have all been assured that the older we get the wiser we get, but I'm not so sure. The only thing of which I am completely certain is that the days go slow but the years go fast. And not just fast, but a whirlwind of flashing scenes and faces when looking back down the dark rimmed corridor of time. Wasn't it only yesterday I asked that pretty little girl to the prom? Why do I remember my first pair of roller skates? My first bike? How is it I remember the names and faces of everyone in my eighth grade class? I think I know the answers. It's because memory works in fast years, so they didn't happen all that long ago. When counted in slow days they happened sometime around the Permian, but that's in slow days. In memory it all happened yesterday.

The days go slow, the years go fast
And soon before you know it
We've watched our time on earth go past
And hope we didn't blow it
We got things right from time to time
That hunting dog, that scope sight
We got things wrong, but that's no crime
We always tried to do right
We try our best, but we're just men
And when we fail we're shattered
We pick ourselves right up again
Though bloody, bruised and battered
We've made decisions that we know
Were not the best we could have
We've done some things that go to show
How wrong we were, or should have
That's not to say that we're alone

In looking back in sorrow
At things for which we can't atone
At least not 'til tomorrow

FATE

An elderly Italian woman missed Air France flight 447 when she arrived too late to board the plane. She escaped death when the plane went down into the Atlantic, killing 228 people, only to die a week later in a head-on collision with a truck on a road in Austria. Events like this raise the question, is it fate, coincidence, or the hand of God, however God is defined. I confess I have not the answer, though I don't believe our fate is written, chiseled in everlasting stone. Nonetheless, there are times I think the ancients had it right, that there are gods living among us, gods who know our fates, gods who shape our lives. In Germanic legend the mistresses of human destiny were the Norns, three spinners; Urd, who knew the past; Verthandi, who knew the present; and Skuld, who knew the future. It is they, the Norns, who shape the destiny of men. And who shall say they do not?

Here is the babe, the women said
In silence as they crept
Into the house and to the bed
Where little Barack slept
But hours old, Verthandi sighed
What know of him, dear Urd?
The past is blank, though I have tried
Of him there is no word
No past? said Skuld, how can that be?
Perhaps, dear Urd, you've missed
The lad's now hidden history
For surely there's a list
There is no list, no proof of birth
His presence unremarked
The lad has simply come to earth

We know not where embarked
But 'tis the future of the lad
With which we must engage
His future now, if good or bad
Dear Skuld, please fill the page
I shall, dear Urd, and you will hear
Him promising much change
I see him bringing hope and fear
And what is passing strange
I see a country bending low
Accepting every whim
I see a people crying so
And all because of him
I see that freedom's lost its way
And men do quake in fright
In hearing what this lad doth say
So say the fates tonight
Is there no hope, can naught be done?
It's written now in stone?
Ah no, said Skuld, they're saved from One
By Ronald Reagan's clone

THE ENGAGEMENT

Bloomberg News reports that the Obama administration will proceed with its plan to engage Iran. The problem is, the mullahs want to be engaged with the United States only so far as it serves their purpose of delaying any action on the part of the US regarding their nuclear program. Once Iran has the bomb, of course, there will be no further need to pretend they welcome engagement with us or anyone else, except to formulate the terms of our surrender. If we're going to get engaged to the lady, make sure it's not a one way street, with us going the wrong way. My advice to President Obama is this:

To be engaged you need a ring
To put upon her finger
But just be sure she's had her fling
And now she wants to linger
With you and only you my lad
And not with Mr. Putin
Or what is worse or just as bad
With someone high-falutin'
Like China's big-time rulers now
Who seem to be so deft
And think it's time we took a bow
And exited stage left
And just be sure she's not a flirt
Just stringing you along
Before she throws you in the dirt
And sings a goodbye song
I see no good from this affair
No matter that she's charming
I say to you just have a care
Some belles are quite alarming

BARNEY

Barney Frank is always an easy target. So whenever nothing significant happens on a given day I trot out old Barney. He serves us lampooners well. Just the other day Barney Frank told a CNBC interviewer, "This interview is over," and stormed away. Or maybe he pranced away. I don't know, I wasn't there. The interviewer was asking him about the Obama administration's plans to determine the proper pay scale for private company executives, which Barney is in favor of. Timothy Geithner, Secretary of the Treasury, says while he is not in favor of the government setting private company pay scales, he believes the shareholders should have a say in what company execs earn. The problem is how to ask the shareholders what that pay should be, since most shares of large publicly held companies are held by major investment institutions. No, if this goes through, the shareholders will not determine executive pay in private companies, the government will, which means guys like Barney Frank and Tim Geithner will decide what the CEO of Microsoft should be paid. I talked this over with a five year old I know and she said, "I love Barney."

She said if I were a designer kid
I'd want Barney for a daddy
I'd love him for the things he did
Though some say he's a baddy
So what he's played the Congress game
'Cause so do many others
What e're he's done it's just the same
As his Congressional brothers
I love him for his winning smile
I love him for his color

You can see purple for a mile
It never gets no duller

When I pointed out we weren't talking about Barney the purple dinosaur but Barney the congressperson, a man who wants to help President Obama turn the country into a socialist paradise, a replica of France, a man who somehow forgot to declare all his income come tax time, a man who never saw a socialist program he didn't like, she thought a moment before replying.

She said they're just like robbers who
Just want to steal our freedom
There is no difference 'tween the two
Just tweedledee and deedum
I like my country like it is
Why do they have to change it
They want to take away the fizz
And really re-arrange it
You say that Barney's not a star?
He's not what I've been thinkin'?
He's not a purple dinosaur
He's more like something pinkin'?
Well just for that I take it back
We'll fit him for some nooses
If I'da known he's just a hack
From lib'ral Massachoosses

Moral: You can fool some of the people all of the time, you can fool all of the people some of the time, but you can only fool a five year old once.

ARE NEWSPAPERS DEAD?

Journalists and TV talking heads bemoan the seemingly bleak future of newspapers and the MSM in general, and increasingly worry that they might not live even in a shrunken state. Much thought is given to the idea that journalists should return to prior times, when journalism was a part time occupation. I don't see this happening, but I do think newspapers and news magazines will return to a prior time when they were an unabashed mouthpiece of a political organization. Everyone knew where they stood, and their readers agreed with them or they didn't read it. People who don't agree with Fox News don't watch it, and people who don't agree with Keith Olbermann don't watch him. Newspapers were not named the Whosis Democrat and the Whatsis Republican for nothing. In this transitional period most of the MSM has already achieved this prior status, and is the mouthpiece of the Democratic party and the liberal point of view. We have not yet seen the rise of an alternate and competitive MSM, but we will.

Ed Murrow sat in smoke filled booth
While Cronkite filled his pipe
They gave us what we thought was truth
Which we now know was tripe
We had forgotten that these guys
Were not the chosen few
But closet liberals in disguise
But then, what else is new
The New York Times was proud to claim
Their news was bias free
The DC Post's one claim to fame
Is that they're from DC

Between them both we got the word
They wanted us to hear
And once we heard we were a herd
And went where they would steer
But we're a whole lot smarter now
We've seen through the charade
We've seen them work and we know how
They manage the parade
They're going now, they're leaving town
Good riddance to the lot
I only hope that while they're down
We kick out all their snot
They've led us now to where we are
At liberal's heaven's door
The constitution no more bar
To things they hunger for
Like socialism for us all
And state run enterprise
But shortly we'll hear freedom's call
And much to their surprise
The people of the USA
Will say enough's enough
You've had your run, you've made us pay
And now we call your bluff
We're taking back our country now
The people we have spoken
We'll put the pieces back somehow
And restore the land you've broken

HOSTAGE

North Korea has announced it will weaponize its plutonium, is preparing for another nuke test, fires off rockets designed to reach the US, and warned that it would consider it an act of war if any of its ships were stopped for inspection, all while the United States looks on impassively. In January 1968, an unarmed US Navy ship, the USS Pueblo, was seized in international waters off North Korea by the North Korean navy. In the attack, one US sailor was killed, and the remaining 82 crewmembers taken hostage. In North Korean jails the crew was beaten and tortured until they confessed to espionage. Eleven months later the United States government apologized to North Korea and the crew was released. One day there will be another Pueblo, only this time it won't be a ship that's held hostage, it will be us. North Korea has hundreds of high caliber artillery tubes within striking distance of Seoul, with hundreds more short and medium range missiles capable of reaching every part of South Korea, including our bases in the south. What's more, this artillery can deliver chemical weapons. Should the mercurial Kim decide to move, some two hundred thousand Koreans will be killed in the first twenty-four hours, most of them in Seoul, and many hundreds of our soldiers. What will we do if he says pay up or Seoul goes up in flames? And if you think that's bad, just wait till he marries his nukes with missiles capable of reaching the West Coast.

> Some say all right, just nuke them now
> While others say why not wait
> They'll change if we just scrape and bow
> And things will then be just great

While others say you're both wrong, still
It really doesn't matter
For what we know of Kim Jong Il
We'll soon be all the sadder
For one fine day he'll smile and say
You think we've all been playing?
It's time to ante up and pay
There is no more delaying
I've got the nukes and missiles too
I'm not afraid to use them
LA, Spokane to name a few
Can you afford to lose them?
You could've stopped me long ago
But dithered and played my game
You had the guns but did not show
The guts and much to your shame
And so I offer you a way
To stop the nukes from flying
And save Spokane and then LA
From instant death from frying
And on that day you'll cringe in fright
And cry out for your momma
As missile trails streak through the night
From Nome to Yokahama

IF THIS BE TREASON

I am becoming uneasy about our Commander-In-Chief. On January 20, 2007, Iranian trained terrorists, dressed in American uniforms, ambushed and killed five American soldiers and captured four. When rescuers closed in the American captives were murdered before the terrorists were captured. Among the captured Muslim terrorists were Ali Mussa Daqduq, Quais Qazali and his brother Laith Qazali, the leaders, the planners and the murderers of American soldiers. President Barack Hussein Obama has just released them, ostensibly for the return of some British hostages, even though the British government refused to submit to hostage blackmail. Have we come to the point where we must question the wisdom, or even unthinkably, the patriotism, of our president? He has sided with the mullahs against the protesters for democracy in Iran. He has slashed defense spending while giving billions to the United Auto Workers union. He has nationalized the automobile industry and much of the banking industry, and is trying mightily to destroy the best health care system the world has ever seen. But it is the freeing of Iranian trained terrorists, ambush killers of American soldiers, murderers of captured American soldiers, that causes me to wonder. What is he up to? Why did he do such a thing? Whose side is he on? Or shouldn't we wonder?

This sort of thing's right up his alley
Freeing killers like Qazali
Siding with the killers of our guys
Selling out the brave protesters
Smiling while the murder festers
Acting like a Muslim in disguise

I'm not sure, I have no reason
Thinking that it's surely treason
Possibly there's something up his sleeve
Something grand beyond imagine
Some grand prize he'll soon be cadgin'
Fooling those poor mullahs who believe
That he's with them and against us
That he's shackled and he's fenced us
Into places where we can't get out
And then when they try something bigger
Obama smiles and pulls the trigger
And all comes down with one enormous shout
The nukes are gone and so are Quds
The bad guys out and in the goods
The rotten Middle East in smithereens
Oh wouldn't it be nice to think
That when it comes it's they who blink
Excuse me while I wake up from my dreams
For I am bound to say out loud
That O and all his lefty crowd
Have taken our fair country round the bend
They've taken up the Muslim course
Who call our death without remorse
And who can tell just where it all will end

The cap and trade bill failed of passage in a heavily majority Democratic congress, but the Obama administration bided its time and as of this writing, with the Republicans in control of the House and the Cap and Trade bill dead, the Environmental Protection Agency has been charged by the President to make cap and trade the law of the land by regulation. So much for a republican form of government. So much for consent of the governed.

CAP AND TRADE

President Obama and the Democrats in Congress are pressing furiously for a carbon tax to fund their outrageous giveaways of trillions of dollars to the unions and other faithful. Of course they don't call it a tax on every single American who lives and breathes and exhales carbon dioxide, they call it carbon cap and trade, and are prepared to convince the unwashed rest of us that the tax won't fall on us but on polluters like the people who supply our electricity. The idea, so they claim, is that the government will set the minimum amount of carbon allowed to enter our pristine atmosphere, and that people who do not reach that minimum may sell their unused carbon credits to people who do exceed the minimum. Also, carbon emitters may buy carbon credits from companies who will plant trees or bloom the oceans, the trees and plankton blooms eating the carbon and thereby canceling out the overproduction of carbon dioxide by the industry now deemed a polluter. Bear in mind that former Vice President Albert Gore owns a carbon credit company, and so stands to make a whole lot of money out of this global warming scam he has done so much to promote.

The environmentalists behind the scam see a bright future in a carbonless world, President Obama and the Democrats see a way to tax their way out of the trillions in debt they have foisted on the country, and Mr. Gore sees immense personal profit. No matter that carbon is the essential building block of all life on earth, and that without carbon life as we know it would not be possible. No matter to the environmentalists, the Democrats and Mr. Gore. Carbon is bad. Oliver Cromwell was once cautioned by a close friend, "For the love of God, Oliver, consider you may be wrong!" William Rutherford, in a paper to the Royal Society, once calculated how much longer the sun would continue to burn by assuming the sun was composed of the finest Welsh coal. Rutherford had the grace to add that the calculation depended on further information about the nature of the sun. Chesterton famously remarked that a man who does not believe in God does not believe in nothing, he believes in anything. And that is where we now are. People who have nothing to believe in now believe in anything. The global warming alarmists have no inclination to consider they may be wrong, for they have an agenda, and are convinced, despite the history of cooling and warming cycles, despite the science, that Western man and Western civilization are destroying the planet, and so therefore Western man and Western civilization must be destroyed. The global warming fanatics who are driving this travesty of science and common sense at least believe the nonsense they are spewing. I'm not sure President Obama and the Democrats believe any of the global warming nonsense, but they sure are trying like hell to take advantage of it by passing carbon cap and trade, and if they succeed, it will be the largest single tax increase on every single American in the history of the country. How did we come to this?

Alarmists say the USA is harming
Earth and little people everywhere
Adding to that awful global warming
Far more than our natural global share
Carbon is the real time big time villain
Carbon's got to go the creatures say
Anybody caught by Feds while spillin'
The stuff into the air will surely pay
But there's a way to keep that old pollution
From making all your profits fall and fade
All you need is formal absolution
By buying into that neat cap and trade
Here is how it works, it's really easy
You just buy credits from the comp'ny store
Don't worry if you feel a little queasy
To learn the company's owned by one Al Gore
We've got to clean the atmosphere in some way
We've got to have clean air and all that stuff
So what if little people lose their payday
You know some people always have it rough
The upside to it is the ones we do please
Envirowhackos and their loopy crowd
Are happy to collect and spend the new fees
What's more our sacrifice sure makes them proud
To think the USA now takes the world lead
In shutting down our fact'ries and our work
To stop the Warming's awful frightful warp speed
They're proud to see that none of us will shirk
In the big fight 'gainst cigarettes and whalers
We're all on board to save good planet earth
From all us fascist CO2 exhalers
Who started breathing shortly after birth

SIEG WHO?

In his few short months in office, President Obama has nationalized the automobile industry, the banking industry, distributed hundreds of billions of taxpayer dollars to his union constituencies, overridden the Constitutional provision of Congressional approval of Cabinet appointments by appointing non-confirmed czars to oversee the Executive department, and passed trillion dollar stimulus bills and bailouts causing trillion dollar deficits as far as the eye can see. Obama is preparing to nationalize the best health care system the world has ever seen, and the House passed Obama's national security force youth bill, heeding candidate Obama's call for a youth group of millions of volunteers, to be equipped, in the president's words, as well as the military. I don't believe he has yet decided on the color green or brown for the Obama Jugend uniforms. In any other country, and at any other time, this would be called fascism, a charismatic autocrat with a rubberstamp parliament. Will we see, in a few months, a hastily called press conference with Robert Gibbs emotionally reading an address to the people of the United States from President For Life Barack Hussein Obama? Will we see Mr. Gibbs cry with unbound joy as the Washington press corps rises as one in thunderous adulation? Will we hear the following words from Mr. Gibbs? "My fellow Americans, I bring you tidings of greatest joy. Our beloved president, Barack Hussein Obama, has proclaimed the following words shall be read and memorized throughout the land."

With whose eyes shall we see the world
There are those who will see the world hollow
With whose mind do we see fellow man

There are those who will tempt us to follow
They will smile and attempt to arrange
Your thoughts and your life and your time
By promising comfortable change
And it won't cost you one single dime
Oh they know how to work it so well
They know every button to push
But know that the road leads to hell
I speak of that road built by Bush
We're now in a crisis, they'll shout
Obama is moving too fast
Only we know what it's all about
The One's promises surely won't last
Yes, that's how they speak ill of us
But we'll save you in spite of your fears
Just know that we're driving the bus
And we'll be at the wheel many years
We're creating a new nation here
A nation we're all proud to serve
A nation we all hold so dear
That we tingle the end of each nerve
Which is why we've decided on this
That elections are truly passé
Now the robe of your Caesar you'll kiss
Though we'll still have an election day
While you won't vote you won't really care
It's the symbol that really does count
With these purple hemmed togas I wear
I'll look swell sitting here on the mount

I'M AL OBAMA BOUND

The Minnesota Supreme Court on Tuesday declared Al Franken the winner of the tightly contested 2008 Minnesota Senate election. Franken won by 312 votes out of 2.4 million votes cast. The election night returns gave the contest to the Republican incumbent, but the narrowness of the victory generated an automatic recount, and the Democrats brought in the man who stole the Washington state gubernatorial election for the Democrat loser a few years earlier by finding uncounted Democrat votes in desk drawers, and he succeeded in finding enough uncounted Franken votes in Democrat car trunks to overturn the election. And so Al Franken is now the junior senator from Minnesota. He will take his seat in the United States Senate in a few days, giving the Democrats a 60 seat filibuster proof supermajority, where they can pass any bill they want with total disregard for the wishes of anyone but themselves.

To the tune of that old ragtime song I'm Alabama Bound.

I'm Al Obama bound
They'll be no filibusters while I'm hanging 'round
Just gave the meanest 'lection man on earth
All I'm worth,
Just to put my tootsies in a Senate berth
Just hear that gavel sound
You know that soon we're gonna cover ground
And then we'll pass all of Obama's dreams
Crazy schemes
I'm Al Obama bound

We end the glorious month of June the way it began, with Congress spending your money in the dark of night, with no one looking.

RUM RUNNERS

Diageo, a London distillery, is the beneficiary of 2.7 billion dollars of TARP money to build a rum distillery in St. Croix, Virgin Islands. All without anyone knowing it was happening. This sort of thing happens all the time, and one wonders what is hidden in the massive and unread stimulus and energy bills about to hit us. What nice little favors did congresspersons add when no one was looking? It isn't as if the average congressperson thinks it's our money. No, it's their money, to with as they please.

It's nice to have good friends in real high places
Like congresspersons looking out for you
Who write you in without the slightest traces
Of what it's for or why it's for or who
They add their little schemers in the darkness
When all believe the gaveled day is through
They understand their colleagues will thus hark less
To what it is that they're about to do
But what is two point seven billion dollars
When calculated 'gainst the greater good
No point in getting hot under the collars
It's just the way things are, that's understood
It isn't if it really were your money
It isn't if you had it in your hand
But if you think this kind of stuff ain't funny
Come 'lection day just tell them go pound sand

JULY 2009. The summer was hot but the housing market was cold. Housing prices plummeted, mortgages were not being paid, underwater homes were being foreclosed and new home construction was deader than a ten penny finishing doornail. Joblessness was up as the home construction industry ran out of homes to build, and the economy in general looked in serious condition. Just about the only good thing to happen in July was the Phillies got Cliff Lee from Cleveland, guaranteeing them another trip to the World Series.

MINNIE THE MERMAID

An underwater homeowner is defined as someone whose mortgage exceeds the value of his house. The Federal government is now gearing up to bailout these underwater homeowners by allowing Fannie Mae and Freddie Mac to refinance those under threat of foreclosure. These types of sub-prime loans were a large part of the housing and subsequent financial collapse in the first place, and Obama's answer to fixing the sub-prime problem is to write more sub-prime loans to people who cannot repay them, or they wouldn't be facing foreclosure in the first place. This strategy will work if the housing market suddenly and unexpectedly enters another inflationary bubble, which is not only unlikely but highly undesirable. On top of that, Fannie and Freddie are already deeply in debt, Freddie having already gotten 50.7 billion dollars from the Federal Treasury, and Fannie 30.4 billion. Of course we know this isn't about underwater homeowners at all, but keeping Fannie and Freddie afloat so they can be looted by Democrat operatives like Raines and Gorelick, who voted themselves millions of dollars in bonuses based on falsified profit statements before the big collapse.

My home is my castle, we heard the man say
So what if the mortgage is due
Obama's my man, he say not have to pay
My mortgage is paid off by you
With Fannie and Freddie behind me I'm set
To live here as long as I want
With Dems now in power I'll take what I get
And if the bank takes it I'll punt
Is this a great country, I'll say that it is
When people like me without jobs
Can buy a new house with some dough that aint his
And live there like middle class slobs
And anyone questioning what's going on
Is seen as a GOP tool
Although to be honest they're wise to the con
It's just that Dems want to be cool
They think that it's awful that people like me
Who cannot afford to pay rent
Are denied owning houses as good as Spike Lee
Even though I don't own a red cent

HOPE AND CLIMATE CHANGE

The House has narrowly passed, with a great deal of arm twisting by Pelosi, the Markey-Waxman climate bill, designed to change our electricity generating plants from fossil fuel to "green" fuels by taxing out of existence the fossil fuel burning energy sources that produce 90% of our electricity. Hydroelectric produces a further 7%, meaning 3% of our electricity is now produced by renewable sources acceptable to the ultra-liberal environmental crowd, including President Obama, who views a climate bill's cap and trade provisions of carbon credits a means of taxing his way out of the enormous debt he has put us in. So the Dems are giving us a choice; either we pay three or four times as much for our electricity as we do now because the carbon tax will be passed on to us, or we do without electricity, because wind and solar cannot provide at any time in the near or distant future 100% of our electricity needs. So President Obama needs a cap and trade climate bill, and the only way he can get it is to insist the climate is changing and we're all gonna die if we don't stop burning coal and oil and if we all don't stop exhaling carbon dioxide.

The climate is changing, we're told by the One
Regardless of facts that it's not
And even if proven we're warmed by the sun
He'd not change his mind by a jot
The icebergs are melting, the bears in decline
The seas are all rising a lot
And even if proven the bears are all fine
He'd not change his mind by a jot
The air is polluted with carbon you know
It's hard to know just what we've got

But even if proven the air's fresh as snow
He'd not change his mind by a jot
He'll not change positions on climate, we're told
He says that it's gonna get hot
And even if proven we're gonna get cold
He'd not change his mind by a jot
For climate's the answer to things that he lacks
He sees it as dough for the pot
And even if shown that it's really a tax
He'd not change his mind by a jot

FROM SEA TO SHINING SEA

On July 2, 1776, the Second Continental Congress, assembled in steamy hot Philadelphia, voted to declare independence from Great Britain. What we know today as the Declaration of Independence, dated July 4, 1776, was a formal explanation of the declaration of independence voted on two days previously.

The American Revolution did not start with the Declaration of Independence, it began more than a year earlier, on April 18, 1775, when the British marched from Boston to Concord, to seize munitions stored there by the Massachusetts militia. The British were met at Lexington by the Minutemen, then by more militia at North Bridge, and were forced to fall back to Boston, where they were besieged. George Washington took command of the Continental Army, and after the battle of Bunker Hill, and with the arrival of artillery captured at Ticonderoga on the hills surrounding Boston, the British abandoned Boston and left for Halifax, Nova Scotia. General Washington then took his army to New York, where he awaited a British attack he knew would come. In July, 1776, the British arrived before New York in force and surrounded Washington's army. When the declaration of independence reached General Washington he had it read to his troops. There was now no turning back, no negotiated peace, no settlement of grievances short of war to the finish.

With the Declaration agreed to and signed on July 4, several broadsides containing various versions of the text appeared in public almost immediately, but the official text, with all the signatures, appeared in the Pennsylvania

Packet on July 8, 1776. The citizens of Philadelphia were the first to read the now famous words

> *When in the course of human events, it becomes necessary for one people to dissolve the political bonds which have connected them with another...*

words that caused many to be uneasy. The war was not going well. Great Britain was the most powerful nation on earth. These words were followed by

> *We hold these truths to be self-evident, that all men are created equal...*

How many who read those words fully understood the impact those few words would have on the history of the United States, the history of the world? There followed a list of twenty-seven grievances against the King and Parliament, justifying the declaration of independence voted for on July 2nd. The Declaration concluded with the following words

> *And for the support of this declaration, with a firm reliance on the protection of Divine Providence, we mutually pledge to each other our lives, our fortunes and our sacred honor.*

There followed fifty-six signatures, including John and Sam Adams, John Hancock, Benjamin Franklin, Caesar Rodney, Thomas Jefferson, and ending with the words, Adopted by Second Continental Congress, July 4, 1776.

And so it began.

Oh beautiful for spacious skies
For amber waves of grain
For purple mountain majesties
Above the fruited plain
America! America!
God sheds his grace on thee
And crowns thy good with brotherhood
From sea to shining sea!

Oh beautiful for patriot dream
That sees beyond the years
Thine alabaster cities gleam
Undimmed by human tears
America! America!
God sheds his grace on thee
And crowns they good with brotherhood
From sea to shining sea!

Katherine Lee Bates, 1895

BAGHDAD BOOB

Do you remember Saddam's comical mouthpiece, Baghdad Bob? Well, we now have Baghdad Boob. It has been revealed that the Iraqi army has been using prostitutes as informants to nab bad guys. Is this news? Is this new? Hardly. Women have been used from time immemorial to gain information that would otherwise be unattainable. A man who would suffer torture and death for not speaking is apt to disclose not only his entire life story but the most secret things of his life when wrapped in the arms of a soft, loving, sweet smelling woman.

Ah yes, the ladies do us proud
As source of information
For men do tend to talk out loud
In such a situation
While lying in a bed so warm
'Longside a charming female
He often cannot see the harm
In telling of his email
From colleague Hamid who that day
Sent him complete instruction
On how to make the gentile pay
And how to sow destruction
Upon the unbelievers who
Would drink and do such other
Things a Muslim would not do
At least not 'fore his mother
The good Jihadist must not think
Of things beyond the warfare
Until it's time for love and drink
With his beguiling whore fair

A QUID PRO QUO

Reuters says Russia and the United States have arrived at a deal whereby the United States will be permitted to ship non-lethal supplies through Russian territory to Afghanistan. At the moment there is no word on what the United States will pay for this largesse, but rest assured, Putin will want something. The question is, what has Obama agreed to give Putin?

We all know what the price will be
It's Georgia Putin wants
Obama says it will kill me
But you can have it once
We move the Braves to Illinois
And shift some other clubs
Though I am sure it will annoy
The White Sox and the Cubs
And then I want, said Putin's smile
Ukraine and Poland too
The near abroad, just for a while
Then given back to you
But not until we've had a chance
To put in place our men
The guys who took us to the dance
And'll take us there again
Done and done, Obama laughed
Done cheaply at the price
Much less than our Chicago graft
And nearly twice as nice
And what we get for what we gave
Just puts my mind at ease
A dozen cans of Burma Shave
And Russian MREs

JAMBALAY AND A CRAWFISH PIE

Ex-president Manuel Zelaya vows to return to power in Honduras, a power he intends to keep, following in the footsteps of his Venezuelan pal Hugo Chavez. The president of the United States has sided with the Honduran left wing fascist who had designs on being president for life and against the people in Honduras who prefer democracy. As the great Hank Williams sang it,

> ManZelaya, a craw fish pie and a fillet gumbo
> 'Cause tonight I'm gonna see my maChavez mio
> When Obama, keep things calm-a, we'll be gay-o
> Son of a gun, we'll make them run, and obey-o

Of course, Hank never dreamed an American president would side with the likes of Hugo Chavez, and demand a would-be dictator be returned to office, which is why his songs were mostly about being lonely. President Obama is never lonely. He has friends in high places, and the only problem for us is that those high placed friends of Obama's are no friends of the United States.

> When looking at Obama's friends
> We see where this is going
> We now see clearly that these trends
> Show where the wind is blowing
> Bowing to a Muslim king
> Who really doesn't like us
> Who really never does a thing
> To catch the guys who strike us
> And then there's Putin who we're told
> Is now best friends with Bama
> Who'll usher us in from the cold

And act as Bambi's mama
The North Korean act is mad
The Chinese act is sly-o
But Obie says it's not as bad
As day old crawfish pie-o

SCAM I AM

Dr. Seuss created a character called Sam I Am. The environmental whackos in particular and the liberal Dems in general have created a character called Scam I Am, and that scam is man-made global warming. All the evidence points the other way, that man has literally no effect on climate, that there have been recent periods of the earth's history when the global temperatures were much higher than they are today, yet global warming alarmists continue to shout for the shut down of the American economy in order to save the planet from their mythical and mystical nightmares. But do they really believe that if we don't act now the world will come to a screeching halt? I don't believe they believe. It is my belief their agenda is the destruction of the western world in general and the United States in particular, in order to rebuild that world in their own wise and wonderful image. They are not nuts, they know what they are doing, and they are dangerous.

Yes, global warming is a scam
But that's not why they try
The lefties only want to jam
Their fingers in our eye
They want the world to be like them
So pure and fresh and clean
And since they're all crème de la crème
Opposing them is mean
But here is my solution to
What they say that they fear
We'll simply shift pollution to
The Eastern hemisphere
Here's how it works, the plan's a plus

That's not been thought before
We'll shift away the stuff from us
Onto a foreign shore
The Western hemisphere declared
Off limits to all kinds
Of stuff that makes enviros scared
And fevers up their minds
We build big fans like we do best
And run them night and day
And have them facing east and west
To blow the stuff away
To change the temps from warm to raw
We change the point of freeze
Then lower all the temps by law
A couple of degrees
Pollution gone and warming dust
That leaves the ocean rise
But as for that I fear we must
Take that as a surmise

FLYOVER COUNTRY

Saudi Arabia has recently given the okay for Israeli planes to fly over Saudi airspace to bomb the Iranian nuclear facilities at Natanz and elsewhere. For the Saudis, this is a no-brainer. It is difficult for us, living in what we think of as a secular age, to believe people of differing religions cannot all get along, but such is the case. The Saudis are Sunni Muslim, and the Iranians are Shi'ite Muslims, and they do not particularly like each other. The Saudis, and all the Sunni Arab states, know that if the Shi'ite Persians get the bomb, the Persian Shi'ites rule the Middle East, which up to now has been a Sunni province. And since the Israelis are the only ones capable of stopping the Persians from getting nuclear weapons, the Saudis are perfectly willing to let the Israelis take care of it for them.

The Saudis say
That on the day
Israelis strike Iran
They might say hey
Or by the way
But never warn Teheran
The Saudis know
That when winds blow
From Persia to the west
It's time to show
The Persian foe
Israeli planes are best
The Saudis think
That if they blink
A Persian nuke will land
And thereby sink
The Saudi kink

And all his merry band
So they're content
To sit their tent
And watch Israelis fly
With their consent
To kill the gent
Who said the Jews must die

Curiously enough, death panels as described by Ezekiel Emmanuel MD, are called for in the Healthcare bill passed by the House and Senate and signed into law by the president in 2010, just in time for it to cost the Dems the House.

PAGING DOCTOR MENGELE

Ezekiel Emmanuel MD, Rahm Emmanuel's brother, has co-authored an interesting article on health care in the Lancet, the British medical journal. Rahm Emmanuel of course is President Obama's chief of staff, which explains why Zeke is now Obama's "Special Advisor For Health Policy", and is currently engaged in the task of turning our health care system upside down. In the article in the Lancet, Ezekiel Emmanuel and his co-authors lay out the various ways of deciding who gets treatment and who doesn't. Part pf their recommendations for the rationed government health care is that the very young and the old get minimal health care, while the productive get taken care of. I think we've seen this one before, and it has always ended in someone in authority deciding who goes to the gas chamber and who does not. Another interesting item is called "Instrumental Value", where again someone in authority decides that someone of instrumental value to society will get treated first. We've seen this one too. The Party bosses get their own hospitals and department stores. Of course, the largest problem in any national health care rationing system is who gets to decide who gets treated, who gets to live, and who gets to die. And we already know who the deciders will be. The deciders will be the politically connected, the liberal elites, the Rahm and Ezekiel Emmanuels of this world.

Well now says Rahmie's brother
We'll fix this thing up right
And soon we'll have another
Little bitty health care fight
We want to make things even
We want to make things fair
That's why we shall be heavin'
Out that nasty old health care
We know right now we have the best
Health system in the world
But we progressives cannot rest
And so the gauntlet's hurled
You've seen the charts you've seen the graphs
You know now what's in store
The young and old get epitaphs
The rest of us will score
Of course we know that some will say
The rich will get the share
That rightfully belongs to they
Who qualify for care
And politics will surely play
A roll in who gets what
The well connected have their way
The rest of you get squat
But best of all we at the top
Already know what gives
We get to say whose life will stop
And get to say who lives

SLIP SLIDIN' AWAY

Rasmussen Presidential Approval Index polling numbers show President Obama losing steadily among voters. The Rasmussen survey uses a plus/minus number derived by establishing the percentage of voters who strongly approve of the president and the percentage of voters who strongly disapprove. The smaller number is subtracted from the larger number to give the poll result. On 11 July President Obama had a minus 7 poll rating, that is, 7 percent more voters strongly disapproved than strongly approved. The decline in approval has been fast and precipitous. On 10 June Obama had an approval rating of plus 9, meaning 9 percent more voters strongly approved than strongly disapproved. In the past month Obama has lost 16 points in the Rasmussen approval rating. Some years ago Johnny Cash sang a song about the crick rising up around the cabin. The lyric went *How high's the water, mama? It's five feet high and risin'.* If you look at the poll results as Johnny Cash would have looked at them, Obama is not falling, the water is rising.

How high's the water, Obama
It's five feet high and risin'
How wide's the water, Obama
From here to the horizon
Whatcha gonna do, Obama
Make the water stop risin'
How you gonna do that, Obama
By something real surprisin'
Surprising how, Obama
By stopping all surmisin'
You mean them polls, Obama
Their meaning we disguisin'

98

Rasmussen truth, Obama
The man just feeding pizen
It don't look good, Obama
Your panic I'm despisin'
How high's the water, Obama
It's nine feet deep and risin'

A WEAKER HORSE

President Obama, against strong advice from his military commanders on the ground, has released five Iranian members of the Revolutionary Guards Qods Force who were captured in Iraq and held by the US military. The Qods Force was responsible for the deaths of hundreds of US soldiers and marines by training and supplying al Qaeda fighters with weapons, including roadside bombs. This comes on the heels of the release by Obama of Laith Qazali and the Irbil Five, who, dressed in American uniforms, ambushed and killed five American soldiers and captured four, murdering the captives when about to be caught. I am getting quite nervous about our president. Economies recover, depressions end, but if the President of the United States is on the other side, we're in big trouble. Of course, there will be those Obama apologists who will patiently explain to those of us who dare question, that Obama's release of killers of American soldiers is in the best interests of the United States.

Some will say now what the hey
Releasing these five Qods
Will just be seen to only mean
Obama's brand new buds
In Teheran will surely plan
To be more kindly for
A week or two and then, who knew
Will show our prez the door
We're now of course the weaker horse
For crawling on our knees
And begging odd Madinejad
To be nice pretty please
And stop the dance and if by chance

You need something from us
We'll gladly send Israeli friend
Under the Persian bus

CAUSE AND EFFECT

Christopher Hitchens has recently wondered if the current unrest in the streets of major Iranian cities after the presidential election there had anything to do with the fall of Saddam Hussein in 2003. Hitchens wrote in Slate, the online magazine, that the Ayatollah Khamenei, the Supreme Leader of Iran, is becoming increasingly isolated, challenged by the former president Rafsanjani, who recently traveled to Najaf, in Iraq, to visit the Ayatollah Sistani, the spiritual leader of Iraq's Shi'ites. Hitchens further states there is a serious undercurrent in the statement issued from the Iranian holy city of Qum, to the effect that President Mahmoud Ahmadinejad has no claim to be the representative of the Iranian people, leading one to wonder if the clerics in Qum are opposed to clerical rule.

The noble Hitchens wants to know
If events in Iraq
Could in their way effect to show
What seems to be the tack
Some certain circles in Iran
Have taken to of late
That caused the unrest in Teheran
That may have been...but wait!
Are not the same guys still in charge
Do not they want the bomb
Does not the whole wide world at large
Look on with pleased aplomb
When Ahmadinejad insists
That Israel must die
Which is the reason he persists
In giving it a try

Whatever stuff is going on
And this is just my take
Is like a child who's blowing on
The candles on his cake
We clap and laugh and cheer out loud
We pat his little head
We make the toddler feel so proud
He made the candles dead
They aren't dead and here is why
The bomb is coming soon
The IAF is set to fly
The first dark of the moon
It's clear to rhymers like myself
The ticking clock's in Qum
I don't need words from off the shelf
They all rhyme with kaboom

OBAMACARE

Life proceeds in stages, and the life of a democracy is no exception. It has been observed elsewhere that a democracy begins to come apart when the public realizes it has the key to the public treasury. That is where we now are, where we have been for some thirty or more years, where a sizeable portion of the electorate expects the government to take care of them, and they vote for politicians who promise to unlock the public treasury for them. Obamacare will be the final nail in the coffin of democracy, for once a socialized government controlled health care system is in place, it will never be removed. Just ask an Englishman waiting months for an operation that will take place in a filthy government run hospital, or ask the fortunate Canadian who can afford to come to the United States for medical treatment. We can avoid the total destruction of our democracy, but only if we band together to stop Obamacare, for once that is in place, the government, which now owns the automobile industry and the banks, will then own you.

Doctor! Doctor! Will you please
Prescribe to ease my pain
I know they've lowered all your fees
And I can't see you again
Until my ration card is stamped
Downtown at Barack's place
So now that our health care's revamped
I cannot show my face
But doctor! doctor! I hurt so
I can't wait for my turn
To see why I am breathing slow
And why my eyes do burn

And why I cannot feel my toes
Or have a cup of tea
Without my wondering where it goes
Is something wrong with me?
What's that you say, I'm now in line
For consultation when?
You say in six months I'll be fine
And you can see me then?
All right if that's the very best
That you can do right now
I'll just go lay me down to rest
And hope indeed somehow
That I can last until that date
Obama says that I
Can see someone to medicate
Sometime before I die

BUYERS REMORSE

Various liberal propaganda organs, like the Washington Post and the Huffington Post, have recently and rather decorously questioned some of the things their hero has done and not done that he has promised to do and not do. There is a small stir in the left-wing blogosphere, where usually tight-lipped ranters are delicately asking if the Messiah has not in fact quite lived up to their expectations. He has not, for instance, to this point surrendered the United States to its enemies as they fervently wish for, nor has his gutting of missile defense satisfied them. His promise to destroy the best health care system in the world looks to be in peril, and his giving of billions of taxpayer stimulus dollars to the unions to insulate them from the perils of the marketplace, while laudable from their point of view, has not as yet accomplished their goal of destroying the evil capitalist financial system that has made the United States the envy of the world. The acolytes are beginning to stir, however reluctantly. Are we seeing the beginning of a serious left-wing buyers remorse?

> Where does hope go when it's gone
> What is left when there's no change
> When will facts then finally dawn
> On his fans that Obie's strange
> Lack of failure up to now
> To enact his promises
> Means that when he breaks a vow
> There're more doubting Thomases
> What's the difference between Bush
> Who the liberals truly hate
> And Obama's Hindu Kush

Where's the policy debate
Yes he's done some things they crave
Like his stripping of defense
And his mighty union cave
And his acts 'gainst common sense
Like his running up the debt
To a height not seen before
But they really do not get
Why he's in that Afghan war
Oh he's still the coolest guy
And the smartest one in town
But they'll tell you on the sly
That he's really let them down

SMOKE 'EM IF YA GOT 'EM

A Defense Department study urged that the US military become tobacco free. Men who go into combat don't care about their health forty years down the line, they care about the next forty minutes. Fortunately, cooler heads prevailed, and the Defense Department insisted it would not implement the no tobacco policy. Anyone who has ever watched an old WWII movie will be struck by the way wounded soldiers would ask the medic or the Padre for a cigarette while on a stretcher, waiting to be evacuated to the aid station.

Yes GIs craved smokes even when they got hit
From Padres who asked them to pray
And nobody said that they really should quit
For they knew they could die the next day
They used them for money right after the war
When nylons and Luckies were king
From whiskey and wine and to ladies galore
It sure beat White Christmas by Bing
When shells were still flying and Tigers still lurked
Round the corner with gun pointed south
And the GI pinned down needed something that worked
Like a panzerfaust punch to the mouth
But the days of the terror and pain were now past
And the ruins of Europe lay waste
And the rations held Luckies or Camels that cast
A glow of contentment and taste
Those days are now distant but memories still
To those who survived to tell tales
Of the battling bastards the Krauts could not kill
Leaving debt much too big for the scales

But that was then. Now there are those who would deny our military the freedom to smoke if they wanted to, even as their Commander-In-Chief, President Barack Obama, admits he sneaks a cigarette now and then. No, today, if you smoke, you are a criminal, a danger to society, to be scorned and vilified by the tobacco police and the sheep who listen to them.

They're against the folks
Who like their smokes
They're makin' them a criminal
But for some blokes
There's different strokes
The lesson here's subliminal
If you're Joe Doaks
The butt of jokes
A redneck like yo mama
You take your pokes
And nasty jokes
But at least you don't sneak 'em like that smiley hopey
changey guy Obama

RED, WHITE AND BLUE HIGHWAYS

The United States is again offering Israel a road map to peace in the Middle East, but is a road map with roads that lead nowhere truly a road map? President Obama met with Israel Prime Minister Netanyahu some weeks ago, trying to convince Bibi to accept the two state solution laid out in the left wing Israel Policy Forum road map for Middle East peace, but the Prime Minister insisted that for Israel to accept the US must guarantee the peace if Hamas takes over the West Bank, which guarantee President Obama was reluctant to give. The road map has no Interstates, only blue highways, twisting and turning, leading down dead ends, heading nowhere in particular.

There is a history here. President George W. Bush offered a similar road map in 2002, but the process goes back further than that, to President Carter and the Camp David Accords, to Oslo, and on to the present day. All these attempts at mediation called for a two state solution, a Palestinian state on the West Bank, and Israel in its pre-1967 borders. The Israelis were and are agreeable to a two state solution, but only if they can be guaranteed the Palestinian state would be a peaceful one. The Palestinians, for their part, have always rejected the two state solution, pushing instead for a one Palestinian state solution, with Israel destroyed and all the Jews dead. A sensible observer might conclude the Palestinian attitude makes any settlement unlikely, but not so the diplomats. To the diplomats, peace is not the end, the process is the end. The end, however, will come with Israeli bombs, for the peace of the world does not hinge on the Israeli-Palestinian question, as the left believes, but on the Israeli-Iranian question, where the only relevant questions are, How soon after Iran has nuclear weapons will Israel be destroyed, and How long can Israel wait before attacking Iran.

A road map can mean many things
To some a way to go
To others though the term just sings
Of peace with one's dear foe
To those of messianic view
The road map shines so bright
That they cannot conceive of who
Could think the thing not right
Two states is surely what the world
Would like to come about
The Palestinian flag unfurled
In Israel and without
But Bibi knows Obama knows
That if he does agree
The danger from Hamas still grows
Despite Obama's plea
That both sides come to friendly terms
Ensuring O's repute
Until the maggots and the worms
Settle all dispute

THE EMPIRE AND THE GLORY

Stuff happens so fast and furiously that it is often difficult to keep up. On July 16 the British Army Chief of Staff, General Sir Richard Dannat, visited British troops in Sangin, Afghanistan, in an American helicopter, explaining that he did so because he didn't have a British helicopter, renewing the charge against Prime Minister Gordon Brown that he has sent British troops to war without proper equipment or support. Back in June Brown's Labour Party suffered a humiliating defeat in the European Union parliamentary elections shortly after being defeated in local British elections. The Labour Party is laying its woes at the feet of Brown, whose gaffe at the D-Day ceremonies in Normandy when he referred to the American landings on Omaha beach as Obama beach did not help matters. Many in British political circles view Gordon Brown as a dead man walking, with the expectation that David Cameron's Conservatives will win the next general election and possibly take Britain out of the European Union. The political life or death of Gordon Brown does not matter to us, but the life or death of Britain does, and the steady erosion of British liberty, influence and power in the face of growing Islamisation, demographic decline and the increasing abandonment of long held western traditions is both saddening and concerning.

The man we know as Gordon Brown
Whose grasp exceeds his reach
Has flickered out in London Town
Despite Obama beach
Whose glistening sand and cheery mien
Have done no earthly good

So now Gord Brown must quit the scene
As we all knew he would
But does it matter to us here
Across the briny deep
For no one has the least to fear
The British lion's leap
The day has passed when who it was
In power really mattered
Her steep decline occurred becuz
Her confidence was shattered
As empire came an empty dream
And socialism's system
Full thrust the labour unions' scream
Down throats that di'nt resist 'em
So now it's gone, that lovely Isle
That source of law and glory
But close our eyes and we can smile
Recounting England's story

THIS IS NOT ABOUT ME

"This isn't about me. This isn't about politics." So said
President Obama on Monday in an online conference
with progressive bloggers, urging them not to lose heart.
"We'll get it done," he said, and by getting it done he
meant the destruction of the finest and most innovative
medical system the world has ever known.

It's not about me, he said with a smile
It's you I am looking out for
You know that my words are quite absent of guile
And my heart weeps for those who are poor
Unable to see a physician when pained
From lack of insurance and such
And answering those who say what's to be gained
I say that we gain Midas touch
For money will pour into Treasury's lap
From savings my health care will bring
And bountiful funds from my carbon tax cap
Will blossom the country like Spring
I know there are some who say I've over reached
They say that my Waterloo nears
Some say that by acting I'll soon be impeached
But friends I shall be here for years
I'll not make mistakes others made in the past
I'll not have my army retreat
Beyond 2016 my office will last
And victory will taste oh so sweet
An Emperor will take what he wants and he's got
An army of zealots to boot
And I with my very own Count Bernadotte
Will have a whole country to loot

ONE AND DONE

A week or so ago President Obama was in Moscow, trying to reset the button in the relations between the United States and Putin's Russia. Russia has agreed to allow the US to use Russian territory and airspace to re-supply our troops in Afghanistan, and one suspects Mr. Putin did not give away this chip carelessly. What is it President Obama gave Mr. Putin for this largesse? We don't know, but I suspect it will be nothing good for the United States. President Obama's entire foreign policy consists of his unalterable belief that his smiley charm will melt the steel cold heart of every dictator he meets, and that by apologizing for the United States and giving up our allies, principles and interests he can remake the world in an image acceptable to him and his radical left wing zealots. We can only hope the cliff he runs us off is not too high.

What else can we say
What more can we do
O's here for another three years
In Moscow one day
Then Ghana, who knew?
He's answered our very worst fears
He likes cutting deals
He thinks that his charm
Will dazzle the Putins he meets
The problem, one feels
He gives up the farm
To every dictator he greets
We know he has smarts
We're told every day
His IQ is real and not feigned
But when he departs

How much did we pay
And what will the Kremlin have gained
A missile shield lost
An ally or two
What matter it's all for the best
So what of the cost
What matters to you
Is that Obie passes the test
What test you may ask
The one Biden claims
Will come to inspire the One
To rise to the task
Or go down in flames
Let's hope that it's not One and done

ONWARD AND UPWARD

The dials on the Debt Clock update the out of control spending at an alarming rate: the national debt; US spending year to date; social security year to date; US government bailouts year to date, and so on. The numbers are staggering. The Obama administration has saddled uncounted generations of Americans yet unborn with massive debt, a great deal of it to pay off his union buddies. Vice President Biden has recently said, "We have to spend money to get out of debt." This is Alice In Wonderland, except we won't be going through a looking glass, we'll be going through economic Armageddon. But I have a solution. Gertrude Stein famously said she and her friends in Paris in the twenties supported themselves by taking in each others' washing. I believe we can sell our pets to each other for huge sums, thereby jump-starting the economy, leading to higher taxes, and thus paying off President Obama's debts and not leaving them to our grandchildren and great-grandchildren.

A dog was for sale for a million
No offers came in and so that's
Why the owner gave up and called Lillian
And traded for two of her cats
One cat was named Miles 'tother Standish
Five hundred thou each was the price
A half a mil each seemed outlandish
But Miles was especially nice
The notion soon gained wide acceptance
That selling one's pets for huge sums
Was the way to get out of the debt stance
And see that economy hums
And so Spot and Fido were sold off

For sums that astonished them all
And pretty soon all debt was told off
And kitties were now put and call
The market chimed in and the Dow Jones
Climbed fast and soon saw record heights
As doggies who only could chew bones
Were sold for their barks not their bites
The collapse when it came came most quickly
As shaggy dogs found their way home
And owners, some pleased and some prickly
Got out the dog brushes and comb
It all ended up in our favor
It ended up nice as you please
With an ending one really could savor
With the bag being held by Chinese

INCOMING

An amateur astronomer in Australia was the first to see the comet slam into Jupiter a few days ago, raising questions about how well prepared we are to detect something big heading our way, and if we did detect it, what could we do about it. Another question is if a large planet killing rock is discovered heading our way should people be told they have x days to live. Some would prefer not to know, others would want a last chance to tell that special someone that they love them. Or would the planet erupt in mayhem as millions of people get even with whoever they have always wanted to get even with. But what happens if the astronomers are wrong? What happens if the comet misses? Can you undo telling your best friend's wife you love her? Can you bring the neighbor who spoke ill of you back to life? Serious questions. And perhaps a more serious question is why are we dependent upon amateur astronomers to find these things?

The amateur the heavens scanned
And then with barely trembling hand
He cleaned the lens to calm his growing fright
A great big rock showed in his 'scope
Mistake, he thought, his only hope
And scanned again to see if he was right
Oh no, he said on second glance
That big old rock sure has a chance
Of hitting pretty close to where we are
And that, his Aussie buddy said
Means pretty soon we'll all be dead
Methinks the thing is quite a bit bizarre
Let's have a look, see what we've got

A little time or quite a lot
Aha! I see we've hours till impact
We'll spend it wisely, you and I
By staring 'tently at the sky
Except for us I'll bet the thing's untracked
Ya think we should alert the press
Inform the public of the mess
About to come our way from outer space
Or should we let them go their way
We shouldn't need to spoil their day
Though perhaps they need some time to die in grace
It's too late now, his buddy yelled
And dropped the 'scope that he had held
And ran about the room in sudden fear
It's on us now and that's a fact
It's minutes now we have to act
And what is worse we're almost out of beer

MOUNT RUSHMORE

Barack Obama's overheated disciples are even now saying that the One deserves to be on Mount Rushmore for his speeches alone, which are, they assert, of transcendent brilliance. Obamaspeech.com offers the text of 100 speeches going back to 2002. The electronic library of his speeches and remarks runs to 36 pages. But will speeches alone, no matter how brilliantly other peoples' words are read from the teleprompter, gain Obama access to Mount Rushmore? The answer is yes, if the Main Stream Media have anything to do with it. On the other hand, for those who believe Barack Obama is a Muslim, the question is will Mohamed come to the mountain or will the mountain come to Mohamed.

Mount Rushmore beckons
But who reckons
Obama will be there
Not I said the hen
Not I said the wren
Nor I said the gentle hare
Mount Rushmore's face
Will take its place
With monuments of old
Each likeness one
Of battles won
Of action brave and bold
Since time began
What sort of man
Used words instead of deeds
To gain the flame
Of fleeting fame

And think that he succeeds
We know of one
A Kenyan son
A master of disguise
But joining those
Whom history chose?
He's not one of those guys

THE FALL

As of this writing Rasmussen shows President Obama's job approval rating at 49% approve, 51% disapprove, down from the high 60s approval rating just a few short weeks ago. RealClearPolitics poll average for Right Track/Wrong Track now shows 36.5% of the people think the country is on the right track, while 55.7% believe the country is on the wrong track. These numbers indicate there is still a chance the country may not be blindly following the Pied Piper down the road to socialist destruction so desired by President Obama and the radical left. The public seems to be rejecting the notion that prosperity will come with gargantuan deficits as far as the eye can see, that crippling the economy with a punitive and completely unnecessary carbon tax is a wise thing to do, that destroying the finest health care system the world has ever known is an exercise in rational behavior, and rewarding unions with billions of taxpayer dollars will stimulate the economy. We have three more years of President Obama, but there is hope now that the country may live.

> The time of the fall
> Is apparent to all
> It comes when the people perceive
> That the God that they took
> For divine is a crook
> And that's when they no longer believe
> When the MSM turns
> And the vast public learns
> The Messiah has feet built of clay
> They will spurn him no doubt
> And demand he be out

And his whole crew of clowns on their way
But of course we all know
That we can't make him go
Till his time left in office is done
He will still be our prez
No matter who says
That the country must shed of the One
Yes that's right girls and boys
Though I know it annoys
All of us to know that's understood
We can only just pray
That we live till the day
That he's turned out of office for good

HIGH NOON

Twenty-two prominent East European figures, including Poland's Lech Walesa and The Czech Republic's Vaclav Havel, wrote an open letter to President Obama, begging him not to forget them in the president's lurch toward Russia. Will President Obama listen to this plea not to be forgotten, not to be cast aside by Obama in his missile defense and other deals with Putin? One has the feeling President Obama has no time for sentiment, no time for allies, no time for long standing friendships, if they stand in the way of his overarching design to remove the United States from a position of leadership to, in his words, just another country in a long list of countries. The plea not to be forsaken must have amused him.

Do not forsake me, oh my darling
She cried and sobbed please come back soon
But in DC with visage gnarling
Obama says it's past high noon
We've got some fish to fry with others
The Russians and some others too
Now Puti-poot and I are brothers
And deals are made that don't count you
The world has changed since last we saw you
Stand athwart the commie tide
And as the bear tried hard to paw you
You stood up for your country's pride
But that was then and this is now, sis
Your days of freedom left are few
I'm sorry that I have to say this
I have to flush you down the loo

VICTORY IS NOT AN OPTION

President Obama, in an interview with ABC News, said he does not like to use the word victory. "I'm always worried about using the word 'victory'," he said, "because, you know, it invokes this notion of Emperor Hirohito coming down and signing a surrender to MacArthur." This is astounding, though not astonishing, given what we now know about Barack Hussein Obama and his utter contempt and dislike for the United States, its traditions and culture. Disregarding the fact known to most schoolboys that Hirohito was nowhere near the USS Missouri on the day in question, it is not clear to me whether Obama thinks surrendering to the Americans was a humiliation to the Japanese not to be borne, or whether it was a personal embarrassment inflicted by vengeful and vindictive white people on a dignified man of color. Whatever, the import of what Obama said is clear. He does not believe in victory. He strove mightily, as did other Democrats, to lose the war in Iraq, in the belief that losing the war would be beneficial politically to Democrats. Which raises the question, what are we doing in Afghanistan? Why is he sending men to die if not for victory?

Victory or death, men used to say
But such words now are quite passé
And victory as such is much deplored
Our president has said as much
And he is surely more in touch
With matters military 'cross the board
Than those of us who seem to think
That when at war one should not shrink
From doing what we need to do to win

So we should follow Obie's lead
And when we fight we should concede
That victory in war's a mortal sin
For enemies that kill our guys
Are merely friends that we may prise
Away from habits warlike, harsh and cruel
And turn them into people who
Believe in all the things we do
And all who don't believe this is a fool
But somehow I can't quite believe
That wearing hearts upon our sleeve
Is quite the way to show them we are right
For in a war you win or lose
And which is not for you to choose
And victory or death be why we fight

FLY OVER

The White House military office recently had a photo op of a backup Air Force One flying over the Statue of Liberty at low altitude, scaring the bejesus out of New Yorkers who remember 9-11. Mr. Caldera, the political hack put in charge of the office despite the fact the office has until Obama been manned by professional military men, has been relieved of his duties. The photo op cost over $300,000, a not inconsiderable sum considering alternative less costly means of getting the shot.

Don't be alarmed, the Air Force said
We won't hit someone's building
All we want from A to Zed
Is just a little gilding
For Air Force One, that special craft
The President must ride in
We know the mission turned out daft
That's nothing we take pride in
We're sorry that some people took
Our flying low for terror
And while we did this by the book
We will admit the error
The man in charge has been dismissed
Thank goodness he's not Air Force
And while it's good that he's been dissed
We've straightened on a fair course
So in the future when we need
That Air Force One go hopping
We'll get our pictures but we'll heed
. That stuff called photoshopping

KA-BOOM TIMES

French workers have taken to holding company executives hostage to further their wage demands, but a recent event at the New Fabris auto parts plant has taken the hostage scenario a step beyond. The workers have taken the factory hostage, planting bombs, and giving Peugeot and Renault until July 31st to meet their demands for severance pay or they will blow up the plant. At least the teachers unions and the United Auto Workers don't hold the schools and factories hostage; they just hold us hostage.

They try to put you in your place
By sneers and shrugs and oft-times little smirks
But when it comes to work place rules
Their union bosses offer duels
To oligarchs who think they own the works
A few days past a shut down plant
Had offered workers just a scant
Amount of euros as their severance pay
The workers took it not too kind
And then they took it in their mind
To bomb the plant and put their plan in play
So now they sit and wait until
The company dips in the till
And count the days as union deadlines loom
They vow if they don't get their way
The company will have to pray
That when they strike the match it won't kaboom

IT'S A LONG WAY TO TARPERARY

You remember Tim Geithner, the big Wall Street honcho who was confirmed as Secretary of the Treasury even though it emerged that he had not paid his income taxes. President Obama dismissed this lapse in judgment as of no consequence, saying Tim Geithner was indispensable to the country, and the only man capable of rescuing the economy from the near bottomless pit it was left in by George W. Bush. Yes, that Tim Geithner. Or rather, *this* Tim Geithner.

Our Treasury Sec he pays no tax
Tim Geithner is his name
He says the IRS expacts
Us all to play the game
According to the rules laid down
By people such as he
Who laugh at those who get paid down
By year or quarterly
The rules all have an angle for
The Sec and guys like him
And guys like Charley Rangel or
The other cherubim
He was confirmed despite the fact
His taxes were not paid
For some the deck is always stacked
And allegations fade
He says he has a plan to save
The country and its folks
He says to shut our eyes, be brave
And tell each other jokes
While he in secret lays the plan
For rolling back the tide

He'll tell us as soon as he can
But now he has to hide
The details from our very eyes
Since we don't have a clue
What those so bright financial guys
Are really gonna do
So what is it we need to ask
Tim Geithner has in store
To pay the bills our only task
Just that and nothing more

But that was then and this is now. Robert Stacy McCain, writing in the American Spectator, tells of Mr. Geithner's escalating war with Neil Barofsky, the special inspector general for the Troubled Asset Relief Program, the bailout that sent hundreds of billions of dollars to such as insurance giant AIG and financial giants Bank Of America and Geithner's pals at Goldman Sachs. Mr. Barofsky has reported that the bailout will eventually total 23 TRILLION dollars, a figure vigorously disputed by Geithner spokesmen. What is more irksome to Treasury is that Mr. Barofsky suggested strongly that Goldman Sachs and other recipients of taxpayer money should be required to report what they did with the funds so that the American people would know the money wasn't being sent down a black hole. With polls showing the American people now believe the Obama administration has bungled the economy, with bailout billions going to political pals, it is a near certainty that President Obama will soon be looking for a scapegoat, and that scapegoat will be the once indispensable man, Timothy Geithner.

"Will no one rid me of this meddlesome priest?"
Cried English king Henry the Second

Words Timothy Geithner must think of, at least
As Treasury's Tarp troubles beckoned
As billions uncounted rolled out the front door
To pals and to all he called friend
An inspector general began to explore
How much it would cost in the end
The numbers he crunched told the story of how
If continued the figures did show
That from mere hundreds millions it stood at just now
Into twenty-three trillions 'twould grow
Obama could see that poll numbers to date
Showed the public would hold him at fault
So in order for him to continue to skate
He'll lock Timmy in Treasury's vault

Somali pirates were much in the news the summer of '09, capturing merchant ships on the high seas and holding the ships and crews for ransom, with nothing, seemingly, to be done about it.

AND A BOTTLE OF RUM

There was a time pirates were hanged when caught. A few months ago a Portugese warship caught a bunch of pirates on the open sea with a boat full of grenade launchers, AK-47s and an aluminum ladder for climbing aboard a passing merchant ship. They caught them, but let them go, because there was nothing in Portugese law that dealt with piracy. Lawyers in Britain have advised the Royal Navy not to capture any pirates lest they seek asylum in Britain. In today's West, pirates have rights just like every one else.

I say we take them at their word
Though some word combos sound absurd
Somali is a word that sings
Trips off your tongue like bluebird wings
But trouble comes when e're I hear
The word Somali placed too near
A word that sounds like government
It's then I sniff a certain scent
That tells me something is not right
And caution forms afore I bite
The simplest thing I guess to do
Is arm the willing merchant crew
Then when the pirate grapnel flies
The first man up the ladder dies

But we no longer hang pirates, we interview them. Scott Carney of Wired has interviewed a Somali pirate, asking when do they decide to kill hostages, who gets to go free, how do they set the ransom price and so on. It turns out the pirates have financiers, just like any other business.

So now the guys have financiers
Who plot out the hijacking
Arranging everything in tiers
And see that nothing's lacking
And hostages are graded for
Ethnicity and value
A white man can be traded for
Whatever they can cow you
Into giving them what they
Think you by george are good for
And so because you always pay
They know what you have stood for
They raise the price in many ways
And we have always paid her
We need to get back to the days
Of old Stephen Decatur

Arriving home late, Professor Gates found he had no house key, and so attempted to climb in a window. A neighbor saw this and called police, who arrested Mr. Gates. Gates later charged the police with racism, claiming they arrested him just because he was black. And so the president of the United States got into it, stating the country needed to be rid of its racist ways, and invited the arresting officer, Sergeant Crowley, to a one on one White House summit on racism.

BLUE MOON

Today, Thursday, July 30th, the President of the United States, Barack Obama, will host an informal beer fest meeting between Cambridge, Massachusetts police sergeant James Crowley and Harvard University professor Henry Louis Gates, Alphonse Fletcher University Professor and Director of the W. E. B. Du Bois Institute for African and African American Public Policy. President Obama and Professor Gates have chosen to live their lives as Black men despite both having White mothers, and will use the occasion as a teaching moment, to show Sergeant Crowley, and the rest of us, the error of his and our White repressive ways. Officer Crowley will be drinking Blue Moon beer, while Professor Gates will be drinking Red Stripe or Beck's. And so, with deep and heartfelt apologies to Rogers and Hart, here is my version of that hit song of 1935, Blue Moon.

> Blue moon, you saw me standing alone
> Without a key to my door
> Outside the home that I own
> And then you suddenly appeared before me

135

The only one who knew that I was Black
And then you heard me whisper please accord me
A little gentleman's respect and slack
Blue moon, you need not taken that tack
There was no need to arrest
Except you saw I was Black
And now you suddenly appear before me
Drinking beer and claiming I was wrong
You say the station people did record me
I say you've got to listen to my song
Blue moon, I have big friends in high places
They've got my front and my back
You'll disappear without traces
Don't mess with me 'cause I'm Black

WE'D RATHER NOT

The Aspen Daily News Online reports that Dan Rather wants the president to appoint a commission to rescue the struggling profession of journalism, arguing that the very survival of American democracy is at stake. Dan Rather is not the only reason the MSM is struggling, but he sure helped push it over the cliff.

In days of old
When men were bold
And readers were not particular
We got the facts
And some attacks
Both flat and perpendicular
When Murrow spoke
We did not choke
And wonder who had paid him
We knew it was
The truth becuz
The living God had made him
The New York Times
For just two dimes
Produced a Sunday paper
That told when bought
What whole world thought
As well as latest caper
But Cronkite's tears
While stoking fears
And tearing down the pillars
Led other guys
To claim GIs
Were hulking, brutal killers
This turned the tide

Of the free ride
Once owned by comp'ny presses
And made us wince
And ever since
We've seen beneath their dresses
They're in the tank
And they can thank
Their plight on one another
As readers flee
Their company
And now they cry for mother
To give them aid
For which they've paid
The Dems in largest measure
They cry the first
Amendment's thirst
For justice is their treasure
So we don't need
The Prez to feed
Their cries for a commission
I say they should
Be gone for good
Consigned to hell's perdition

AUGUST 2009. The recession deepened, and people began to think the worst was yet to come.

BROTHER CAN YOU SPARE A DIME?

Bloomberg reports that the Department of Commerce now believes the first 12 months of the recession was twice as bad as previously thought. Are we heading deeper into recession? Does the staggering debt load the Obama administration has strapped to the already overburdened backs of the American taxpayer portend even worse economic news? Are we heading for a 1930s rerun? Does anyone remember what that was like? In 1931 Bing Crosby sang Brother Can You Spare A Dime. We have changed the lyric somewhat.

They used to tell me he was building a dream
And so I followed the mob
I thought that I was really part of a team
And so we gave him the job
Once I built a factory and I made it run
We made cars all the time
Now he's given it to the union and they're having fun
Brother can you spare a dime
On the campaign, gee we looked swell
Full of that Yankee Doodly Dum
Marching with Acorn, giving them hell
And I was the kid with the drum
Say don't you remember, we called him Barack
It was Barack, Barack all the time
Say don't you remember, Barack was our pal
Brother can you spare a dime

GOODBYE GRAMPS

House Blue Dog Democrats are reluctant to embrace the Obama health care scheme because they got badly burned by voting for the Cap and Trade carbon tax that was later shot down in the Senate, leaving them politically vulnerable back home, where the districts they represent are majority Republican. With Obama sagging in the polls, and the public increasingly opposed to Obamacare, it looks like Obama's desired destruction of the finest health care system the world has ever known is on hold, at least for now. The public is well aware that nationalized health care means rationed health care, which the government will spin as efficiency and savings, and rationed health care means many will die who would otherwise have lived. Like grammom and grampop.

Efficiency and savings are all that we crave
Which is why we suggest you die now
And of course we will speed you to your waiting grave
And our doctors will tell you just how
Just lie down be comfy and smile while we work
It's over in just little time
A needle, a pinch, you will find we don't shirk
Just remember you're not in your prime
And what is more sir please remember that you
Voted straight Democrat in the Fall
So needless to say you're the head of the queue
With the line stretching far down the hall
We really don't like offing gents of your age
But it's for your own good, really, Dave
The road that you're taking is now all the rage
And the signs will all read Burma Shave

A YELLOW DRESS

In August of 1983, Senator Benigno Aquino, the leader of the opposition to the dictator Ferdinand Marcos, was murdered on Marcos's orders as he stepped off the plane upon his return to the Philippines under safe conduct from exile in the United States. Cory Aquino, a simple housewife, became the rallying force against Marcos. In the presidential election of 1986 she ran against Marcos, and although Marcos was declared the winner in a fraudulent election, Cory Aquino was installed as the 11th president of the Philippines by the peaceful 1986 People Power revolution. A tiny lady in a yellow dress had toppled one of the world's most oppressive dictators. During her term as President, 1986 to 1992, she gave to her country a new Constitution that guaranteed liberty and human rights for all. She died August 1st, 2009, of cancer, and is buried in a simple grave next to her husband. Three hundred thousand people lined the twelve mile funeral procession, many in yellow shirts or dresses.

The woman who in yellow dressed
Confounded those who would attest
That might makes right and force will rule the day
She had no ships, no guns no tanks
And yet the world owes her its thanks
For showing us that courage is the way
And now she joins the chosen few
The ones who stood for what they knew
Was right and just, with light that lit the world
That shone in every darkened place
Where diktat dared to show its face
And gave her country freedom's flag unfurled

SOMETHIN' FISHY GOIN' ON

The White House blog, The Blog, in a post by Macon Phillips called Facts Are Stubborn Things, asks people to notify them of posts or people they deem to be spreading untruths about the Obama health care proposals. Mr. Phillips writes, There is a lot of disinformation about health care out there. Since we can't keep track of all of them here at the White House, we're asking for your help. If you get an email or see something on the web about health insurance reform that seems fishy, send it to flag at whitehouse.gov

Notice that the White House now refers to the intended destruction of the most successful medical system the world has ever seen as "health insurance reform", tempting us to believe they intend a minor tweak, nothing to worry about. Move along, folks, there's nothing going on here.

'Tis but a step, with whispered smile
He said, To catch what's fishy
To having all the names on file
Whose politics are squishy
Those folks who dare to disagree
With things that we are doing
While on this little spending spree
That some think is ungluing
The country that was forged in pain
And sacrifice and valor
And seem to think that there's no gain
In bleeding down to pallor
All once held dear by all who claim
To love the country dearly

And yet will not accept the blame
For poor health care that yearly
Causes deaths and broken dreams
While costs are nearly tripling
And tea parties with right wing teams
Are very nearly crippling
Our plans to take this country down
The road to wrack and ruin
Those folks outside this DC town
Don't know what they are doin'

IN THE SHADOWS

Obama says his health care plan offers a public option, whereby anyone who wishes to keep his current health care plan may do so. This is a Trojan horse, and everyone knows it. Barney Frank has stated publicly that the public option is a necessary first step toward a single payer system, the single payer, of course, being the government. The whole thing is a shadow play. Barney Frank knows, and we know, that the public option insurance companies will soon be driven out of the health care coverage business by a government run insurance company. The liberals are hoping to fool us with sweet-talking reasonableness, but we know them. They lurk in the shadows. They will never cease their attempts to turn the United States into their vision of utopia, a socialist state with them in charge.

In the shadows, in the dark
They lurk in hidden mist
They know that we're the redneck mark
They know they've got the fist
And when by chance they're in the light
And somehow truth they speak
We see at once that we were right
Their purpose is to sneak
Their socialist agenda on
Us unsuspecting slobs
Who will not know that freedom's gone
Along with all our jobs
But 2010 will soon be here
And with it a new day
We'll sweep the bastards never fear
And see them on their way

AIN'T GONNA PRACTICE WAR NO MORE

John Brennan, head of the White House security office, says that the administration will no longer use the term "war on terrorism", but from now on will use the term "at war with al Qaeda" exclusively, explaining the change was the result of Mr. Obama's views being "nuanced, not simplistic; practical, not ideological."

I have had my disagreements with President George W. Bush, the greatest being his inability or unwillingness to call the war what it was, a war declared by Arab and Persian Muslim terrorists in 1979 against the West in general and the United States in particular, and everything it and we stand for, opting instead for the mushy non-descriptive War On Terror. So while there was a war on terrorists, I agree with the Obama administration on this one thing, that there never was, nor could there be, a war on terror. Terror was simply a tactic in the terrorists' war against us. What I fear is that the Obama administration, in declaring the war on terrorism dead, will also, as a matter of nuance, quietly declare the war on terrorists also dead.

Brennan says the war's against
Those known to be al-Qaedas
And all the others we have fenced
Are simply freedom fightahs
That's why we're closing down the clink
In Cuba where we hold 'em
If we're nice to them we all think
They'll show their hands and fold 'em
Iran now we think is a plus
Elections there are crookit

But Acorn does the same for us
It works and you can book it
The Norks can seize our womenfolk
And hold them both for hostage
We get them back for pigs in poke
Don't watch us make the sausage
Nuance is as nuance does
The world is just our plaything
And we'll continue thinking fuzz
Until it's that doomsday thing

THE WORM OROBOROS

The Associated Press has announced that it will be outsourcing content to leftist non-profit groups, including the George Soros backed Center for Public Integrity. The question is, will any readers recognize the difference between the new left-wing scribblings and the leftist stuff the Associated Press has been distributing under the guise of news for many years.

The AP knows that guys like Soros
Are like the worm of Oroboros
Who swallow their own tails to circle fate
Who live for strife and confrontation
Whose only thrill and stimulation
Is seeing that their enemies deflate
The worm now sees that time is fleeting
That crises meant to keep hearts beating
Are running out of time and out of space
As mobs of grannies storm the barriers
Of Obie's red flagged banner carriers
All shouting No! in Barbara Boxer's face
And so the AP in extremis
Turns to Soros and their scheme is
Not to give us news that's straight and true
But to show their liberal nation
They will keep us in our station
But what they surely know is they are through

CLUNKERS R US

Well noted for their catchy acronyms, the Federal Government has instituted the CARS program, Cash Allowance Rebate System, which attempts to stimulate the automobile industry while at the same time healing the perceived by the left sick environment. The bill authorizes car dealers to offer up to a $4,500 rebate to buyers who traded in their clunkers for more fuel efficient models. The program allocated a billion dollars for this purpose, which was supposed to last four months, but which lasted 4 days. The Congress has now added another 2 billion to the program, which, if recent history holds, will last about 8 days. But the problem is not that the government underestimated the number of people who would take advantage of the program, it is that the government has mandated that the clunkers, many in good running condition, be utterly destroyed. This has the direct consequence of reducing the inventory of used cars available to those less fortunate souls who cannot afford a new car, and by interfering in the market, the government has made used cars more expensive. But the fact that poor people will have to pay more for a used car is quite beside the point to the government, who are congratulating themselves on a program that will, they believe, reduce the carbon footprint those poor people are inflicting on the planet by driving used cars, defending themselves by pointing out that while used cars may be more expensive for poor people who need them to drive to work, the government has also addressed and solved that problem by substantially reducing the number of jobs there are for poor people to drive to. So from the point of view of the Obama administration, this is a win win situation.

There's nothing wrong with a nice trade
That takes cars off the market
You get a nice car newly made
And have a place to park it
And even though some low class slob
Could use some transportation
To get him to his low class job
The government's creation
Of this fine plan will lead to more
Clean air on this fine planet
And show those clunkers out the door
At least that's how they plan it
Of course we know all guv'mint plans
Lead down to deep perdition
So I intend to keep my vans
Regardless of condition

DUMB AND DUMBER

Bill Maher, a self-described comedian, says America is a stupid country, full of stupid people who are too dumb to know what's good for them, meaning, of course, that we are too dumb to appreciate the genius of Barack Obama, not to mention the genius of Bill Maher and his fellow lefties. The leftist, as always, thinks he is smarter than those who are not leftists. The Democrats always characterize Republican presidents, like Eisenhower, Reagan and Bush, as stupid, so having a lefty like Maher call you dumb puts you in good company.

The wit and wisdom of Bill Maher
Is simply quite delicious
I do believe he is a star
Though clearly meretricious
I mean that in its nicest form
He's lost in his pretensions
Believing he is but the norm
Of intellect's dimensions
He thinks we're dumb and more or less
Too stupid to be trusted
To vote for now just let me guess
The guys who just now busted
The bank and socialized the cars
And now will do to health care
What LBJ by lowering bars
Forever did to welfare
I could go on about Bill Maher
With words right on the money
But even looked at from afar
Was he ever really funny?

HOPEY CHANGER

Never let a crisis go to waste, even if you have to manufacture the crisis yourself. If your aim is to destroy an entire country and culture, best to do it while the iron is hot. And best to do it while the mainstream media is on your side, telling people what you want them to hear, what you want them to think. You are the Messiah, the Chosen One, the bringer of Light, and Hope and Change, the creator of a new age of perfection and enlightenment, a brilliant post-partisan, post-racial age, where the wolf and the sheep shall lie down together. And you, oh golden one, are the wolf.

All hail the One, the Hope and Changer
Bestow upon him laurel wreaths
Accord to Him birth in a manger
Blessed be the air He breathes
Purple hemmed the robe He's wearing
Golden sandals tread the floor
Ruby rings of worth past caring
Smiling smiles we all adore
Happy is the land He rules o'er
Happy are his subjects too
Happy teachers run His schools for
Happy children who on cue
Clap and sing we love each other
Clap and sing we love Barack
Clap and sing we love Big Brother
Never get our country back
Hail the One, the Hope and Changer
Bestow upon Him laurel wreaths
Clap and sing for there's no danger
Blessed be the air He breathes

I LIKE HIM

Polls indicate that President Obama's policies have fallen below fifty percent approval, while his personal popularity has remained high. This seems a contradiction, so I asked a woman why she liked Obama. She thought a moment, then said:

> Obama brings us hope and change
> He makes me feel so very strange
> I like him
> Obama brings us change and hope
> The dreams he dreams are vast in scope
> I like him
> I know the country that we knew
> Will be no more when he gets through
> But lordy how I'm telling you
> I like him

But will the Obama presidency change for the worse the country we knew? Will the country we knew be no more? I suspect if we keep our heads we can keep the worst from happening. A man I know, who voted for him, expresses the beginnings of doubt.

> Obama brings us hope and change
> And though his plans are off the range
> I like him
> Obama brings us change and hope
> And while I'd not give him more rope
> I like him
> Of course we'll have to rein him in
> To keep the country like its been
> With luck he'll not be Ho Chi Minh

I like him
But then when I think of the crimes
In other places other times
What he'll do now will surely pale
With what will happen if we fail
To guard our liberties and homes
So when the writers write their tomes
About the times we live in now
The people then won't scrape and bow
And sing Obama, Father's Son
We know you surely are the One
And though my doubts have now begun
I like him

A COMFY LITTLE NOOK

Mr. Peden, a schoolteacher from Topeka, Kansas, has redeveloped an abandoned intercontinental missile base into upscale housing, former missile silos once alive with men and hydrogen bomb tipped missiles now turned into comfy homes. Word is the silo homes are selling briskly.

I feel so safe when underground
Though it's taken me a while-o
To get used to the lack of sound
In my new homey silo
Except at night in deepest dark
I seem to hear some ticking
And distantly a watch dog bark
And Geiger counters clicking
Along 'bout dawn, say three or four
I sometimes hear a rumble
Like opening a far off door
And distant voices mumble
And in my dreams I see the keys
Slide firmly in position
And turn in twain with practiced ease
And then the shout, "Ignition!"
It's then I wake up in a sweat
And thank the guys who manned it
And turned away the dire threat
In times that did demand it
I'm glad that Atlas played its part
In keeping us from frying
Thanks to the crews who from the start
Kept freedom's flags a-flying

NON-SEQUITOR OF STATE

Hillary Clinton, Secretary of State, has a positive genius for saying and doing the wrong thing. In Kinshasa, the Congo, she flew into a rage at a question about her husband, and in Nigeria she said the 2000 US presidential election was stolen. This is not her first display of incompetence for the job. We all remember her fabulously successful visit to Mexico City early on, when she visited the Basilica of Our Lady of Guadalupe, a major Roman Catholic shrine. The story of the shrine is that in December, 1531, an Aztec convert named Juan Diego was visited on the road by the Virgin Mary and told to build a church on the site. The bishop demanded a miracle to prove his story, and the Virgin Mary caused Spanish roses to bloom. When Juan Diego handed the roses to the bishop, they fell from Diego's apron, revealing an image of the Virgin Mary on the apron cloth. The cloth with the image is on display and the object of deep veneration. When shown the cloth she asked who painted it, and was told God painted it. Hillary Clinton is ignorant and churlish, her recent actions possibly understood as a reaction to her realization that she is Secretary of State in name only, dispatched to completely irrelevant parts of the world while the real work is done by others, further magnified by the realization that she was played by the Obama people in order to get her out of the way for 2012.

At the Shrine of Guadalupe now
Our Sec of State let out as how
The Virgin's image was so nicely painted
When told that God had worked the brush
She had the grace to primly blush

155

Then saw the painter's name and promptly fainted
It makes you wonder what she'll do
When faced with other people who
Believe in God and other things she smirks at
She doesn't seem to have much sense
Of how her act has consequence
For country and department that she works at
She snaps at question 'bout her hub
Whose glowing press just seemed to rub
Her in the hardest place she had to scratch
She's sent to places in the past
That State would surely think the last
Darn place on earth the Sec they would dispatch
So now she's really in a snit
She knows she's truly out of it
The president and all his men have shown
That they have made her Sec State queen
To get her off the year 12 scene
And now her presidential chance has blown

MARX AND ANGLES

In the Washington Post, Marxist professor Gregory Clark argues that the wages of unskilled workers have peaked, and that to keep social peace the government will have to tax the productive members of society to subsidize the unproductive. Isn't this what we are doing now? Has Professor Clark not heard of the welfare check? The heart of his argument, however, is that the number of unskilled will continue to grow, and that, in his view, is both problem and opportunity; a problem in that there will be many millions of unproductive workers to feed, and an opportunity in that those millions of hungry mouths provide the opportunity to impose a Marxist solution. To people like Gregory Clark, The Communist Manifesto of Karl Marx and Friedrich Engels is the solution to all our problems, no matter how disastrously wrong that manifesto has been in the past.

What the good professor doesn't say is that the growth of uneducated unskilled workers is publicly unstated government policy, whereby a debased educational system and an immigration system that invites millions of uneducated and unskilled third world people into the country with promised and delivered benefits leads to a permanent underclass dependent upon the government hand that feeds them. This benevolent and beneficent hand, to which is attached the Democratic party, is thus, by the votes of these dependents, locked into eternal power, and with eternal power comes the ability to extend the hand or ball it into a fist.

The muted songs of meadowlarks
Give way at dusk to firefly sparks

And deep in dark the tree frog sings hello
I lay inside my ten room shack
And thank the lord that Marx is back
So those above take care of us below
It's not my fault these working hands
That gathered corn and shoveled sands
Are idle in this workless world of ours
Where unskilled workers such as I
Have not the chance to share the pie
And so I sit and stare at walls for hours
My wife and kids they do all right
The gummint check just came tonight
I figured out what's best for me and mine
I've got the angles covered now
No more a life behind the plow
With Marx and angles we'll be doing fine

HEADS I WIN, TAILS YOU LOSE

President Obama's new Chief Diversity Officer of the Federal Communications Commission, Mark Lloyd, has called for private radio companies to pay licensing fees equal to their entire operating costs. Naturally, National Public Radio will not be required to pay this diversity licensing fee, since the entire purpose of this extortion is to drive conservative talk radio into extinction. President Obama insists he is not in favor of the Fairness Doctrine, yet appoints a man to oversee the infusion of left wing views into privately owned radio stations who is ferociously in favor of it.

To ask the question why do Dems
Our freedoms like to crush
Is answered because we have gems
Like Hannity and Rush
And they have no one like the guys
And gals who're on our side
And so to no one's big surprise
They need to set aside
The Constitution's guarantee
Of free speech for us all
By claiming that it isn't free
If their side cannot call
Upon a host or two or more
Who can an audience hold
Who doesn't make the listener snore
Who doesn't leave them cold
They claim they simply can't abide
Unfairness done to them
By having only on their side
The entire MSM

A MEDIAN IQ

Recent reports of distracted drivers killing themselves and others because they were texting while driving underscore the necessity of having basic intelligence testing for drivers. If it were just a matter of nominating these people for the Darwin award for removing their DNA from the gene pool, that would be okay, but they tend to take others with them. Passing a simple IQ test should be a requirement for obtaining a drivers license, with failure to achieve an acceptable IQ score reason for denying the license, or at the very least requiring the posting of an easily recognizable bumper sticker. There should be plenty of left over Obama stickers, and it may be the IQ test is unnecessary, an Obama sticker on the car in front of you sufficient warning of intellectual incapacity.

It seems to me the deadly dance
Of texting while in drive
Is playing with the odds on chance
That you won't be alive
To get a message back from whom
You sent the message to
For you in your vehicle tomb
Are slowly turning blue
Of course we know the IQ score
Of those who text en route
Is in the rank of fair to poor
And Democrat to boot
So blame it on yo lefty mama
When you're a median jumper
We know you by your big Obama
Sticker on your bumper

WHEN ALL THAT'S LEFT IS LOVE

Camille Paglia, in Salon, lists all of the stupidities, lies and general incompetence of Barack Obama, yet she still loves him. Why? The answer is she loves him not for what he has accomplished, but for what he is - a leftist like herself. Belonging to the same club is enough. Women in particular love Barack Obama because they see him as handsome, cool and caring. He cares about the things women care about, or they think he cares because he says he does. Soft things, emotional things, or at least emotional to women. The hard things, war and national defense, are not in the same emotional world as that populated by most women, who want someone to help them care for their children, someone to substitute for the dominant and, in their view, domineering male they would otherwise have to depend upon. Snug and warm in the cocoon of leftist thought and deed, women will not leave the nest, for that would isolate them from their leftist friends, and no one wants to be alone.

I love him so, she sighed and blushed
So handsome and so cool
No matter if our freedom's crushed
And jackboot Nazis rule
I wouldn't like to see them here
The Nazi thugs I mean
But things like that I never fear
With Barack on the scene
He loves us so, we love him back
He gives us such a thrill
I grieve to see the Right attack
His every little bill
Of course I think it likely that

161

We'll change the country's mind
About this little healthcare spat
And recognize how kind
Our president and Congress are
And how we need them so
And how we need to have a czar
For every little woe
That ill befalls us womenfolk
When facing life alone
And which is why we never joke
About the scary tone
That comes out of the White House now
And causes us some pain
But nonetheless I tell you how
We love our man Hussein

TANGLED UP IN BLUE

Bob Dylan, the legendary folk singer and writer, responsible for such hits as Blowin' In The Wind, The Times They Are A'changin', Rainy Day Women, Tangled Up In Blue and more, was walking around the Jersey shore town of Long Branch the other evening in the driving rain, just whiling away the hours looking at houses until time to go on stage with Willie Nelson and John Mellencamp at the Lakewood Blueclaws baseball stadium, when a 24 year old female police officer, called by a resident who saw him in her backyard and thought he looked suspicious, asked him his name. The name Bob Dylan meant nothing to her, nor did it for a backup 25 year old male officer. Without ID, Dylan talked the police into taking him to the hotel where the tour was staying, where he was identified to the satisfaction of the police officers. My problem with this is not that young police officers did not know who a disheveled, rain-soaked 68 year old folk singer was, but that he was asked for ID because the police said he was acting erratically. That alone should have convinced them he was telling the truth. How else would you expect Bob Dylan to act if not erratically?

I lived with them on Montague Street
He said to responding police
In a basement down the stairs
I will admit to some caprice
But puzzled someone cares
It's pouring rain, the policeman said
You're wandering about
You seem to have it in your head
That we your word do doubt

You say you are Bob Dylan who
Is with a touring band
Along with John and Willie too
All known throughout the land
I've heard the name Bob Dylan as
A boy I am afraid
And I recall my mother has
His records that she played
And you look nothing at all like
The album cover pics
And why would Dylan take a hike
In these New Jersey sticks?
I'll sing a song, Bob Dylan said
To prove to you I'm real
All right, get in, and watch your head
The cop said, it's a deal
And in the car Bob Dylan sang
About a man who sinned
With windows down the clear notes rang
A-blowin' in the wind
And then he sang one for the cops
He said, this one's for you
And fair among the falling drops
Came Tangled Up In Blue

AN OFFER THEY CAN'T REFUSE

The United States has shifted its emphasis in Afghanistan from closing down the opium trade to controlling who runs it. Attacking the poppy fields led to too much local opposition. Killing the guys who control the drug trade and replacing them with more amenable drug dons not only does not annoy the poppy farmers, but puts us in charge of the operation. By declaring we have no problem with drug lords so long as they don't belong to Al-Qaeda or the Taliban, we have enlisted on our side a group of people whose self interest it is to see us win. And that is all to the good.

So now we get to pick and choose
Just who's to win and who's to lose
I like it
The poppy fields will now be ours
Those gorgeous fields of bright red flowers
I like it
Of course with all that dough at stake
We know who'll be in on the take
And though their thirst it will not slake
I like it
The Taliban without the cash
Will have to dig into their stash
I like it
And Afghan rulers on the sly
Will see their source of income dry
I like it
Our man Petraeus is a fox
He thinks of things outside the box
He'll fake these guys out of their jocks
I like it

BRASS KNUCKLES

Henry Waxman (D-CA) and Bart Stupak (D-MI), sent a letter to 52 health insurers requesting financial records for a House committee's investigation. The letter warned the health insurers that the House Energy and Commerce committee was examining executive compensation and other business practices of the health insurance industry. This is clearly political intimidation, and if a Republican controlled House committee tried such a thing the MSM would never let us hear the end of it. But the display of Democrat brass knuckles barely merited a mention in the lap-dog press. But there may be more to it than simply trying to get the health insurance providers to stop opposing socialized health care. It is always possible the congresspersons are looking out for themselves.

Now let me see, the Chairman mused
Faint smile upon his lips
It seems to me that you've abused
Our taking little trips
On corporate jets to places where
There's girls and money too
And while that's neither here nor there
I'll tell you what I'll do
I'll overlook a little bit
Your opposition now
And tell you how I think you'll fit
Into our plans somehow
We may be forced to have a look
Into your books you know
To see if you, by hook or crook
Are playing with the dough
But with your help we can avoid

Unpleasantness and strife
You know the President's annoyed
And you may say that's life
But come on board with all his men
Support his plans right now
And we can take your jet and then
Have fun in Curacao

REAL MEN, REAL WOMEN

Why do women love a TV drama called Mad Men, set in the 60s before radical feminism and political correctness changed what the culture thought of "he-men". The answer might be that women love the bad-boy lead character because they have always loved the bad-boy, always loved the guy with the hairy chest, always loved the guy who slapped them around. Political correctness may play in the lefty media and culture, but real women have always loved real men, and always will.

Pocketa pocketa pocketa
The mighty airship sang
Sailing free and fearsome in the sky
Below him Walter Mitty saw
The fleeing pirate gang
Led across the bay by Captain Bligh
The bomb bay doors flung open then
The airship lurched and breached
The bomb fell clean upon the men
As seagulls flapped and screeched
Where have they gone these mighty men
Have airships disappeared?
Do pirates now use GPS
Are Zulu foes still speared?
We haven't gone, we're here to stay
Though they may curse our likes
We still work hard, and women play
Behind us on our bikes

ZEALOTS

Mark Steyn clarifies the debate over health care saying Sarah Palin's remarks about death panels resonated in a way that rationing never did. The health care bill approved by the Senate Health, Education, Labor and Pensions committee provides federal grants to state and local governments as well as to a national network of community organizers (read ACORN) to promote healthy living, reduce disparities, and to monitor people's weight, eating and exercise habits. (Pages 382-387 of the bill posted on the committee's website.) And why should it end there? If allowed to come to pass, Obama and his radical left-wing agenda will result in the destruction of the United States as we have known it for the last two hundred plus years. The only question is, where will they put the camps for the obese and the dissidents? Who will manufacture the Zyklon B?

For non-WWII buffs, Zykon B is a cyanide based insecticide used by the Nazis in WWII to kill Jews and other people they considered undesirable. The insecticide came in pellets impregnated with a warming substance, so that when exposed to the air it released hydrogen cyanide, a deadly gas. The Nazis herded a couple of thousand naked people, the old, the women and children, into the gas chambers where the doors where locked and a guard on the roof emptied a bucket of Zyklon B pellets into a shaft. The people inside took 20 to 30 agonizing minutes to die, after which the bodies were carted to the crematoria. Will the Obama left go that far? The history of Nazi Germany, Communist Russia, Communist China, the Khmer Rouge and others shows that the Left always goes that far.

Little Johnny's overweight
It coulda been something he ate
It coulda been he got his momma's genes
It doesn't matter to the One
What's good for father's good for son
He's got to know what health care really means
His daddy now admits he smokes
That second hand endangers folks
And since this is the second time he's sinned
His punishment is durance vile
Where he can contemplate the style
In which our organizers sniff the wind
Now mommy she is neither fat
Nor smokes and we are thankful that
She stays within herself and keeps the rules
Our Acorn people say that she
Is quite delightful company
And spies upon the kiddies in the schools
We're getting there, we're on our way
To having all the folks obey
Each rule and regulation and decree
We have the plans and specs to build
The camps upon the land we've filled
Now all we need is cans of Zyklon B

WHAT'S THE BUZZ?

A commenter at Belmont Club thinks there might be some money to be made by selling people on the idea that the Earth's magnetic poles are shifting, just as they've been sold on the nonsense of man-made global warming to the vast financial profit of Al Gore and other conmen. The idea is to sell refrigerator magnets to the gullible, with printed instructions on how to keep them properly oriented for maximum effect upon the poles, and to offer pole shifting offsets just like carbon offsets. Making up stories about Canada geese no longer migrating because of the shifting poles will get the enviros and other whackos rushing to buy magnets. If Al Gore can get a Nobel Prize for nonsense, why can't honest guys like us?

Hey guys we're on to something here
You name the place I'll bring the beer
A TV blitz with crying baby geese
We'll cut Al Gore in for a slice
Although on TV 'twould be nice
If Al would show up not quite so obese
Refrigerator magnets scream
A con man's everlasting dream
Instructions printed all with large size type
We'll get some academics too
Who for a price will work with you
And generate some full time good time hype
I see it now, the dough is real
We're millionaires, a tingly feel
It's gonna be just great I know becuz
Ideas like this come so rare
They just electrify the air
I'm tingling now at thoughts of all that buzz

A MORAL OBLIGATION

President Obama has invited a group of pastors, rabbis and other religious leaders to support his healthcare proposals by claiming it is a religious duty and a moral obligation to do so. "I know there's been a lot of misinformation in this debate, and there are some folks out there who are frankly bearing false witness." But who is doing the lying here? Who is bearing false witness? The people who claim that socialized medicine will not kill grandma with death panels, will not result in piling on more massive debt, will not lead to rationing of health care? The ones who claim the insurance companies are evil? We know who is lying here, we know who is bearing false witness. Were the religious leaders swayed by the theatrics, by the smile, by the smooth teleprompter delivery? Were they astonished when President Obama walked on water?

Across the Galilee they rowed
Arriving tired and sleepy
Above them teleprompters glowed
The stone stage dark and creepy
They stirred with fascination as
The waters rose around them
Celestial angels singing jazz
As Acorn bands surround them
And then as trumpets fiercely blared
And lightning filled the sky
There came the One, the One who cared
Arriving on the sly
By walking on the watered stones
A grin from ear to ear
And from the crowd the roaring tones

Of vast celestial cheer
Then Obie raised his hand in peace
And said to quiet crowd
"My Father's wonders never cease
He does what I've allowed"

THE BIG PARADE

President Obama has appointed almost three dozen czars, making an end run around the Congress and neutering the Cabinet Secretaries (just ask Sec of State Hillary Clinton). These people have enormous power without any accountability to anyone except Obama. This comes very close to Diktat governance. No one knows what they are doing, and apparently that's just the way Obama likes it.

Here they are: Afghanistan Czar - Richard Holbrooke; Aids Czar - Jeffrey Crowley; Auto Recovery Czar - Ed Montgomery; Border Czar - Alan Bersin; California Water Czar - David J. Hayes; Car Czar - Ron Blum; Central Region Czar - Dennis Ross; Climate Czar - Todd Stern; Domestic Violence Czar - Lynn Rosenthal; Drug Czar - Gil Kerlikowske; Economic Czar - Paul Volcker; Energy and Environment Czar - Carol Browner; Faith Based Czar - Joshua DuBois; Government Performance Czar - Jeffrey Zients; Great Lakes Czar- Cameron Davis; Green Jobs Czar - Van Jones; Guantanamo Closure Czar - Daniel Fried; Health Czar - Nancy-Ann DeParle; Information Czar - Vivek Kundra; Intelligence Czar - Dennis Blair; Mideast Peace Czar - George Mitchell; Pay Czar - Kenneth Feinberg; Regulatory Czar - Cass Sunstein; Science Czar - John Holdren; Stimulus Accountability Czar - Earl Devaney; Sudan Czar - Scott Gration; TARP Czar - Herb Allison; Technology Czar - Aneesh Chopra; Terrorism Czar - John Brennan; Urban Affairs Czar - Adolfo Carrion Jr; Weapons Czar - Ashton Carter; WMD Policy Czar - Gary Samore.

Do we really need a Sudan Czar? How about a Czar for Switzerland? An Urban Affairs Czar? Didn't we used to call them Mayors? A Czar for the Great Lakes? What's he gonna do, make sure they don't freeze over in the winter? Isn't that the job of the Climate Czar? This is obviously designed to place Obama's radical lefties between the people and the Congress, the better to rule by Diktat.

Cheer the marchers! Wave the flags!
See the Czarmen marching strong
Dozens of them, no one lags
Marching to a Sousa song
'Bamanation on display
Clad in their Brooks Brothers
Proud they are this proudest day
Prouder than all others
Swinging past the grandstands soon
Grinning oh so clever
As the band blares out the tune
Czars and Tripes Forever

SHEIK, RATTLE AND ROLL

Walter Pincus in the Washington Post tells how Khalid Sheik Mohammed broke under interrogation and spilled the beans, going so far as to conduct terrorist tutorials for CIA intelligence officers, describing Al Qaeda methods, personnel and plans, the information provided keeping the United States safe from terrorist attack since September 11, 2001. This sort of thing is unacceptable to the American Left, as represented by the elected leadership of the Democratic party, who are preparing a witch hunt and show trials for the CIA officers who dared to do their duty, screaming all the while of torture and desecration of the good name of the United States. Waterboarding is not torture; pulling out fingernails with pliers is torture. Sleep deprivation is not torture. Tying someone to the rack and pulling him apart is torture. Drilling into teeth is torture. Sawing off someone's head, as was done to Daniel Pearl by the good Khalid Sheik Mohammed, is torture. What the radical Left is doing to our country is torture, and the question is, will we recover?

The shaken head, the small moué
The frown that says don't do it
To waterboard means we are they
And we will live to rue it
So spake the left, those gentle souls
Who shake with firm conviction
That he who with the devil bowls
Is living life as fiction
No matter that the goodly sheikh
Was harmed not by the 'boarding
The torture road will only make

His words not worth recording
With wroth filled eyes they shake their fists
And scream with indignation
And set about compiling lists
Of those who serve the nation
With boundless rage the lefty crowd
Sets out to hurt the good guys
They plan to leave no one uncowed
It doesn't matter who dies

In late August 2009 it looked like Obamacare was dead. Boy, were we wrong. Obama pulled a rabbit out of the hat. Or was it a skunk? Obama got his victory, but a lot of Democrat congressmen are no longer around to share the high fives.

OBAMACARE KAPUT

Once out of the closed door sessions in the House, once out of committee and into public view, Tea Parties and other demonstrations have indicated to the Obama administration that nationalized single payer Obamacare is dead. There are simply not enough Democrat votes in the Congress to pass it in its contemplated form. The Blue Dogs are running scared and the far left has vowed not to vote for anything if the Public Option is taken out. For this reason Obama has scaled back and is now pushing for insurance reform. It is not yet clear what this will entail, but if he signs a bill that removes pre-conditions and allows the market to set the fees, it will be a good first step toward realistic health care reform. And if he also miraculously defies the trial lawyers and gets tort reform, the country will be much the better for it. Tort reform looks like a non-starter for the Democrats, but even minimal insurance reform will be welcome, and Obama can trumpet it as a victory. But Obamacare is dead, possibly for all time, though that's what Harry Truman thought when he buried the Henry Wallace Stalinist wing in 1948 only to see it rise from the ashes 20 years later in the person of George McGovern and take over the party.

I'm so relieved, the patient said

178

I thought they'd given me for dead
But now I see I'm kicking once again
I'm on my feet and feeling fine
I'm pleased to say that me and mine
Are once more in the land of laws not men
We raised ourselves in righteous wrath
We showed our congressmen the math
And said we would not take this lying down
At Tea Parties we let them know
That they no longer run the show
That we won't sell free lives to DC town
And now Obamacare is done
And he no longer is the One
Who whistles and the pack does what he says
We knocked him down a peg or two
And let him know that you know who
Says take that stuff and stuff it in your fez

SSN SAINT NICHOLAS

Strategypage reports the Russian navy has named its newest nuclear submarine after Saint Nicholas. Do Russian boomers now deliver toys instead of missiles? Do the missile warheads now contain candy and confetti instead of thermonuclear destruction? Has the bear gone all cuddly?

Once upon a midnight dreary
Conning tower wet and slick
Santa rested, sad and weary
Bundled up like old Saint Nick
Seas a-pitching, quite precarious
Sack askew, his step unsure
Reindeer smirking, how hilarious
Periscope a distant lure
"Hold on there, boys," the old man cried
"I've barely time to have a look
Though goodness knows I've tried and tried
To find that gosh darn address book!
This sure ain't no forsaken roof
I think we're on a submarine
Just look about you for the proof
I'm getting soaked and getting mean"
For warmth the reindeer stamped their feet
And shivered lightly in the rain
For hours now they'd faced defeat
As Santa tried the hatch in vain
"I'll get in now, and I do mean
I'll get in now, by Jiminy!
The problem is, a submarine
Just doesn't have a chiminy!
They need a house," he cried aloud

His arms thrust upward to the sky
"A house of which they can be proud
The best that gold can freely buy!"
Up popped the hatch, up popped a head
"I surely know the very one!
There's lots of room," the stranger said
"And lots of early morning sun!"
"And who are you?" the old man asked
"And how did I get on this tub?"
"Why I'm the man who's rightly tasked
To captain now this lovely sub
So come aboard, it's Christmas Eve
The crew and I are waiting
We heard you land, could not believe
And started celebrating
Just follow me right down this hatch
Be careful with your prizes
I see your bag has quite a batch
Of wonderful surprises"
"Can Santa down a hatch go, boys?"
The old man asked his reindeer
"Is it fair wide for bags of toys
And Santa's favorite, Cane beer?"
The reindeer pawed, their heads they shook
They didn't know the answer
"Why don't you just go have a look?"
Piped up the one named Dancer.
He did just fit, though it was snug
And clambered down the ladder
He gave his beard a gentle tug
And said, "It doesn't matter
It's Christmas Eve and every one
Is eager for some cheer
I've something for each mother's son

Including some good beer"
Then through the missile room he stepped
Amid the crew's hubbub
As Christmas morning slowly crept
And blessed their little sub

9067800R0

Made in the USA
Lexington, KY
25 March 2011